W9-BLU-937

Praise for
Touchdown!

"Just as one individual makes a difference, so can one book make a difference. If you follow what it teaches, you will be in a much higher place and get what you deserve, which is victory."

Butch Davis, former Head Coach of the NCAA Champion University of Miami and current Head Coach of the University of North Carolina

"Kevin Elko played a huge part of putting Rutgers Football on the map. We use what he has taught us every day in our coaching. We owe him for teaching us 'The Chop.'"

Greg Schiano, Head Coach, Rutgers University Football

"Dr. Elko taught me 'You have to dream it to achieve it' and that before championships and pro bowls happen, they have already occurred in your mind. From the moment I learned it I have not only played that way, I have led that way."

Ed Reed, All Pro Safety, Baltimore Ravens

"Over my career at the University of Miami, I learned a lot of lessons from Kevin that helped lift myself and my teammates to a higher level. His creativity with his teachings, and the fact that what he taught us worked, was a major reason I still believe in what he taught me to this day."

Ken Dorsey, Quarterback, Cleveland Browns, and former Quarterback of 2001 University of Miami National Champions

"Over the course of my career, the principles that Dr. Elko taught were instrumental in me being a starter in the NFL. These principles are now still what I teach to my athletes in the weight room."

Tom Myslinski, MS, CSCS, Head Strength & Conditioning Coach, the Cleveland Browns Football Club

"If I had one choice for someone to work with my firm, I would pick Kevin Elko. He has a unique way to touch people to become the kind of person they were meant to be. When I need a plan for growth, Kevin is my first call."

Andy Kalbaugh, CEO, Mutual Services (LPL Financial)

"What Kevin has taught us, and you will learn from this book, is that attitude is a muscle, not a gene. Most people do not recognize that a positive attitude needs to be exercised and strengthened every day, so use this book like a gym. I am an optimist—and as they say, there has never been a statue erected for a cynic, and I have never seen anybody drown in their own sweat. This book will teach you how to exercise your way to a positive attitude and work your way to what you desire."

Phil Casparius, Head of Sales and Distribution,
Morgan Stanley Wealth Management

"Kevin's message says two things loud and clear: (1) The best way to predict your future is to create it, and (2) You can have anything you want as long as you pay for it. Understand those two concepts, and you can win."

Wayne Chopus, Vice President, National Sales Director,
The Hartford Financial Services

"Success starts with a dream, no matter how outrageous it seems at the time. If you are going to dream, why not dream Only Big Dreams."

Steve Pederson, Athletic Director, University of Pittsburgh

"Kevin has taught our team at Pitt how to keep their eyes open to small opportunities—he calls it 'looking for crumbs.' This book will open your eyes to the opportunities in your life."

Dave Wannstedt, Head Football Coach, University of Pittsburgh

"Every time Dr. Elko talked to us, we stood up and sang, 'This Little Light of Mine.' Imagine an entire football team singing and dancing to that song—that is how we started every time he visited us at North Carolina. Inside me there is a light as well as those around me. If you understand you must bring the light out that is in you and help others bring it out of them, then you will know the recipe for victory—that is the message Doc delivers."

Kentwan Balmer, Defensive Tackle, First Round Draft Pick,
San Francisco 49ers

"Kevin's ability to connect through stories, logic, and humor moves individuals to confront what's right in front of them. Having a clear picture is the first step to taking action. Truly, a master of communication!"

Jeffrey McGregor, President, RiverSource Distributors

Touchdown!

Touchdown!

Achieving Your Greatness on the Playing Field of Business (and Life)

Kevin Elko

Vice President, Publisher: Tim Moore
Associate Publisher and Director of Marketing: Amy Neidlinger
Editorial Assistant: Pamela Boland
Development Editors: Russ Hall, Zachary Moore
Operations Manager: Gina Kanouse
Senior Marketing Manager: Julie Phifer
Publicity Manager: Laura Czaja
Assistant Marketing Manager: Megan Colvin
Cover Designer: Alan Clements
Design Manager: Sandra Schroeder
Managing Editor: Kristy Hart
Senior Project Editor: Lori Lyons
Copy Editor: Bart Reed
Proofreader: San Dee Phillips
Senior Indexer: Cheryl Lenser
Senior Compositor: Gloria Schurick
Manufacturing Buyer: Dan Uhrig

FT Press offers excellent discounts on this book when ordered in quantity
for bulk purchases or special sales. For more information, please contact
U.S. Corporate and Government Sales, 1-800-382-3419, corpsales@pearson-
techgroup.com. For sales outside the U.S., please contact International Sales
at international@pearson.com.

First Printing July 2009

ISBN-10: 0-13-701960-2
ISBN-13: 978-0-13-701960-1

Pearson Education LTD.
Pearson Education Australia PTY, Limited.
Pearson Education Singapore, Pte. Ltd.
Pearson Education North Asia, Ltd.
Pearson Education Canada, Ltd.
Pearson Educación de Mexico, S.A. de C.V.
Pearson Education—Japan
Pearson Education Malaysia, Pte. Ltd.

The Library of Congress Cataloging-in-Publication data is on file.

*This book is dedicated to my children,
Claire and Jared.
I had a vision of what you two would be, but
you both are so much more.
Thanks for all you taught me.*

Contents

TEN

Speaking Out:

About the Author

Dr. Kevin Elko is a nationally renowned performance consultant and motivational speaker. He has consulted with dozens of professional and collegiate athletic teams, including LSU, Miami, Nebraska, the Pittsburgh Steelers, and the Dallas Cowboys.

He has also worked with companies including Travelers Insurance, Smith Kline Beecham, Prudential Securities, and Tyson Foods. In 2005, he was the top-rated speaker at the Million Dollar Roundtable, a meeting of the insurance industry's highest achievers.

Dr. Elko's books include *Nerves of Steel* and *Winning the NFL Way*. Elko holds a Doctorate in Education with emphasis in Sports and Counseling.

Foreword by Butch Davis

I once read that most people can be changed from a relationship with one person. This is exactly what happened in my relationship with Kevin Elko. I had heard about him from several people in the National Football League, specifically his work with the Pittsburgh Steelers. He was known as someone who could help you identify and select players with a great attitude and leadership ability. When I took over as the head coach of the University of Miami Football program, having players with a great attitude and leadership abilities was exactly what we needed; in fact, the program was in such disarray that year that there was a *Sports Illustrated* cover article calling for the University of Miami to drop football. All the way around, we had many challenges—and if we did not have a plan to overcome these challenges, we were doomed.

We decided our problem at Miami was culture. We had inherited a culture that was producing ineffective results, so we quickly decided to rid ourselves of that culture and to develop another.

Whether you realize it or not, every team—and for that matter, every business, family, and individual—has a set of attitudes that they live by, and that collection of attitudes is the culture, and that culture brings whatever "results" you are getting. It is not something "out there," such as the environmental conditions that give or take away, but rather something "*in* there" or in *you*, that brings about the quality of your life. Therefore, at Miami we developed a vision and mission statements of what we wanted those attitudes to be; and our day-to-day operation was not to win, because winning is a by-product, and winning would take care of itself. Our vision was to keep moving toward that culture with the attitudes we had set for ourselves and to be relentless in focusing on those desired attitudes that positively added to the desired culture. It was that simple.

Now more than ever before, this is an important concept. Today there is a belief out there that is becoming more and more popular that *someone else* is going to do it for you, and this entitlement is going to be spread around. In the short term that idea may happen, but to buy in to this kind of thinking over the long term will hurt the believer of this idea. One concept Kevin has repeatedly taught our teams is, "You never get what you want, but you always get what you deserve." If you work hard and develop your gifts that were given you, and you have a vision of serving and helping others, then what do you deserve? But if you do not work hard on yourself and are not concerned about those around you, then what do you deserve? America was founded on hard work and serving others. This vision and mission will help you receive more. Not only did this way of thinking help the University of Miami win more than 30 straight games and bring respectability back to the program, it developed a record number of first-round draft picks for the National Football League.

Another winning culture-developing concept Kevin brought to us was to "Keep planting grass, and don't pull weeds." We had our share of weeds. We were also faced with a limited number of college scholarships and we were on probation, so it was very important that we made wise choices in the selection of our players. We constantly reminded ourselves, "Keep planting grass." In other words, we knew we had to stay focused on what we wanted and keep doing the things that would bring positive results instead of focusing on what was wrong and the negatives. It took some time, but our players and staff completely bought into this concept. This overall culture eventually became one of the longest winning streaks in college football history. If you're not careful, it's easy to focus on the negatives and all the things you don't have instead of the opportunities that you do have. Another name for this way of thinking is fear. Individuals who think this way need to understand they are helping to bring about that fear. As Job 3:25 states: "For the things I greatly fear come upon me, and that of which I am afraid befalls me." If you focus on what you do not want, it becomes a self-fulfilling prophecy and manifests itself in your world. When we started at Miami, it would have been easy to focus on the things that we did not want.

There were other culture-developing concepts that Kevin taught us, such as, "Never look at the scoreboard"; "Accept accountability"; "If you trust you may be disappointed, but if you do not trust, you will lose"; and one of my favorites, "Sipping on battery acid, chopping down trees." These things, repeated over and over and then reinforced by me and my staff, became the eventual winning culture of my teams in Miami These same concepts are taking hold and having a huge positive effect for myself, our staff, and our players at the University of North Carolina.

This book teaches those concepts of vision and serving in an enjoyable read. I have often told Kevin that, other than my wife and son, he has been one of the most influential individuals in my life. It is not just his lessons but also his friendship over the years. Just as one individual makes a difference, so can one book make a difference. If you follow what this book teaches, you will not need anything "spread around" to you, because you will earn what you deserve, which is victory.

Butch Davis
Head Football Coach
University of North Carolina at Chapel Hill

Foreword by Jon Dorenbos

I grew up in a "Brady Bunch" kind of family. My mom volunteered at the school, and my dad was the president of the little league and a consultant for Microsoft. But life as I knew it would change drastically as I carpooled with the Harper family to a baseball camp on August 3, 1992. At lunchtime Coach Bill Stubbs told me I had to leave due a "family emergency." The Harpers were there to pick me up and escort me to the police station. Officer Childs was at the station, waiting. He was the D.A.R.E. officer at my elementary school, and I overheard him say, "I know Jon; I want to be the one to tell him; I know him, and I knew his mom." He walked over to me with his eyes watering and head slightly looking downward. As he approached me, he lifted his head and said, "Your parents had an argument and your mother didn't make it. We're not sure what happened, but we think she was pushed down the steps. Your father is in jail and being held for questioning." The reality was that on August 2, my parents got into an argument that moved into the garage. There, my father beat my mother to death.

After my father was convicted of second-degree murder, my sister and I spent a year and a half in foster care before moving in with our family in southern California. My brother and I went months and sometimes what felt like years without talking. In one night, life as I knew it was stripped away. I lost my mother and father, and everything in life I was sure of was destroyed and betrayed.

I have learned that there is only one way to overcome a nightmare, and that is with a dream. When I was 13, I saw a magician named Michael Groves. He was 16 and a friend of a friend's family. He taught me my first magic trick and bought me my first magic book, J.B. Bobo's *Modern Coin Magic*. Magic became an escape for me. It was something that I could practice and use to forget about my problems. Little did I know that learning magic as a kid would lead to believing in magic as an adult. I eventually met another magician, Ken Sands, who taught me never to be arrogant with magic, instead to cherish it and to use magic as a tool to create a relationship with your audience. I loved it.

Then I got another dream. I watched Ken Griffey, Jr., Jay Buhner, and Omar Vizquel play baseball for the Seattle Mariners as a kid. I always wanted to play for the Mariners. Sure enough, after moving in with my Aunt Susan, in California, I was going to attend Pacifica High School, home of the Pacifica Mariners. All I could dream about was playing professional ball. I played baseball, basketball, and football in high school. But after my senior year, I was determined to make it in football. I went to a junior college, and after my freshmen season…still no scholarship. So I decided to create an opportunity. I sent in someone else's "game-tape" to colleges, claiming the snapper was me. He was a 6'6" tight end who was a phenomenal long snapper. UTEP got the film and offered me a full ride. The only problem was I was only 6 feet tall and not a tight end or a long snapper. Being that I was recruited to snap, I quickly learned and started for UTEP for the next three seasons. I guess I figured it out well enough, because at the end of my senior season, I got a call from the Buffalo Bills, offering me a chance to try out. There, I met someone else who shaped my life.

Growing up watching the Seattle Mariners, I went to as many games as possible. After the games, I would wait by the players' parking lot, lean against the fence, and watch them drive away. They were "gods" to me. Eleven years later, against the St. Louis Rams, I would drive into the players' parking lot for the first time. As I got out of my car, I noticed a little boy leaning against the barricade. It was then and there that my entire life flashed before me. I was running late and had to head to the locker room. After the game the little boy was in the same spot. So I walked over and introduced myself, "Hi, I'm Jon. What's your name?" He looked at me with his hands in his pockets and said shyly, "I know; you're the magician. I'm Joey." I smiled and asked if he had ever been on the field. He hadn't, so I snuck him and his dad down on the field at Ralph Wilson Stadium. As his father watched him run around, the father started to cry. He explained that Joey had a rare form of cancer and three months prior was given only six months to live.

Joey and I became friends and I tried to include him in Bills' events. One day he asked me if

I wanted to go to the Super Bowl. The Bills weren't that good that year and I told him, "Of course, but it ain't lookin' good this season." He laughed and told me he had tickets and wanted to invite me. I was thinking the Make a Wish Foundation. Instead, Joey reached into his backpack and pulled out two tickets made out of construction paper—one for me and one for him. About a month later I got a call from his dad, asking if I could head to hospital because Joey wasn't doing too well. He told me to bring the tickets. Sure enough, when I got to the hospital and looked at the tickets, in crayon was written the date October 18. As I walked into his room, he smiled, looked up at me and said, "You made it. Today is the Super Bowl." October 18th was six months and one day. Joey dreamed of that day, the day that the doctors didn't think he'd be alive, and to Joey, that day was his Super Bowl. That is what I call having a dream to overcome a nightmare. He had a lot to do with teaching me what is in this book; the child is father to the man.

While I was with the Bills, I met Dr. Elko, who reiterated to me something I already knew, but something I needed to continue learning and continue to cherish. It is something I need to hear over and over. First, we must dream again and again, outrageous dreams, and when we do, nightmares fade. This book opened my eyes, reminding me to stay focused, to stay determined and to stay on top of my game. Reading Dr. Elko's inspiring words are a reminder that dreams don't happen over night. They take hard work and sacrifice. But dreams are worth the work; they are worth the sacrifice, the blood, the sweat, and the tears. Nothing "worth it" comes easy. This book also teaches us that "giving back" is the best way to say "thank you" to all those who have helped us achieve our dreams.

Today I play in the National Football League, and I am about to marry the woman of my dreams. Most importantly, I work to help W.I.N., a foundation that assists abused woman, and many other charities helping children. I love going to orphanages and hospitals to perform magic. It is there that the true magic of life comes out. It's the magic of helping, the magic of lending a hand to those who need it, just like friends and family did for me when I needed it most.

One day I asked my position coach what time it was, and when he looked at his wrist, he screamed, "My watch is gone"; then I handed him back his watch (an old magician's trick). My coach didn't find that trick as amusing as I did. In fact, he looked at me and said, "You think that trick was good? If you screw up on the field, I will make you disappear David Copperfield style."

Sometimes the truth hurts, but once you accept it, the truth can be your friend, and that truth keeps me improving and keeps me focused everyday. And believe me, as soon as I lose focus and stop doing what I'm suppose to do, they will make me disappear. And I'm not talking about my coaches; I'm talking about life.

I have heard Dr. Elko speak a number of times, so today I am delivering this message. Every time I hear him speak, I say to myself, "Yes." The message in this book is one that hits the heart and soul. Live to love, love to dream, and give joy and inspiration back to world. I love Dr. Elko's message. As the commercial says, "Try it; you'll like it." THE DOC ROCKS!

Jon Dorenbos
#46, Philadelphia Eagles

Preface

This is a terrific book. My hope is that you read it, practice the principles you find here, and make a great life for yourself. The world needs you to be successful. *Touchdown!* can help a lot. I'd like to tell you how and why. So please take a few moments and read on.

I used to be an ad man in Australia. My mother and father had been artists—of the mostly starving variety, as I liked to quip. Before I was born, my dad went off to the Second World War where he was injured. He was shipped back to Australia, and after a little while he died. My mom did the best she could, but I didn't have to be psychic to know we were poor.

Being a reasonably bright lad, I figured that the solution to being poor was to make money, which as far as I could tell back then, was the only reason to get an education and endure going to high school and then on to college. The thing about going to college, as compared to going to high school, was that dropping out was less of a big deal in the 60s. So I dropped out and put my creative genes to work as an advertising photographer and creative director. Turned out I loved it and was really good at it. Which was just as well—in today's world, not graduating from college is a seriously bad idea.

Since I'd convinced myself that the secret to being happy was to acquire and consume the right stuff, being a creative type in advertising seemed like the perfect career choice. Basically, I became the guy telling you that if you wanted to have a great life, you pretty much had to acquire and consume the right stuff—and that would be our client's stuff. I was the guy telling you that things actually went better with Coke, that if your deodorant failed your life would, and that if you didn't use my client's toothpaste you wouldn't even get kissed, let alone have a chance for anything else you were hoping for later on.

Then one morning I woke up and realized I had solved the problem of being poor. I had enough stuff to start my own world. Next I reasoned that if having enough stuff was going to make me feel successful and happy on the inside, it would've worked by now. It hadn't. And it didn't seem like more stuff would work any better. So I dusted off my college philosophy and psychology textbooks and began to realize that living successfully had to happen on the inside before it could happen on the outside. Then one day I came across a copy of *Look* magazine. The issue editor, George Leonard, was talking about a thing called the Human Potential Movement happening in California. It was about people transforming their lives. Sounded like just what I needed. He reported that San Francisco was Ground Zero. In Australia it was the summer of '70. I made plans.

I got on a Qantas jet in Sydney and got off in San Francisco. I found myself standing on the corner of Haight and Ashbury. I said to myself, "Self, you are definitely not in Sydney anymore." I got involved with the kind of ideas and practices Kevin is offering you in this book. I became the first CEO of a transformational training company known in those days as **est**. Tens of thousands of people participated. Today the company lives on as Landmark Education. I moved on to co-found an international training company called Actualizations and became a successful partner in a corporate consulting firm. I have written four books—all bestsellers. It's been a wonder-filled adventure.

I know that you really can make it happen for yourself on the playing field of business (and life) if you really want to. First, as Kevin will show, you make it happen on the inside—in your heart and in your imagination—then you make it happen on the outside and become a success in the world. This is one of the core ideas of this book—that it all happens before it happens: First you create a vision for your life, then you take skilled, spirited action. Sometimes this can take awhile. And then suddenly it happens for you in the world. People may even think you're an overnight success. As Kevin likes to say, "It all happens over a long period of time all of a sudden."

A problem with many so-called self-improvement books is that while they might make sense on some level, how to actually take the words off the printed page and put them to work is not terribly clear. Not so with *Touchdown!* The printed pages that follow are filled with Dr. Kevin Elko's crystal-clear messaging and step-by-step "how to." You will be able to do what he suggests and make a rich difference in your life. In the lives of others, too.

As you read this book, you will learn that extreme makeovers start inside your head. Kevin tells you exactly how you accomplish all this. Now, I don't mean to suggest you need an extreme makeover the way I did way back in the early 70s. However, each and every one of us has the opportunity to be more tomorrow than we were yesterday; and the world really needs that from us right now. Always has.

I have learned that the happiest and most successful people in the world have this in common: They discovered what they love to do and learned how to get really good at it. They create tremendous value in the world. Become one of them. If you are already one of them, this book will help you to help others become one of them. This is important work.

I wish you a wonder-filled life.

Stewart Emery
San Francisco, California
April 2009

Introduction

*"Self-trust is the first
secret of success."*

—*Ralph Waldo Emerson*

I was finishing my internship with the United States Olympic Committee when I got a phone call from Tom Donahoe, the head of player personnel for the Pittsburgh Steelers. He wanted me to meet with Dick Haley, Tom Modrak, and him, all three of whom were working in personnel for the Steelers—and would go on to have fabulous careers in the NFL. I flew into Pittsburgh and we met on Christmas Eve. The occasion marked the end of head coach Chuck Noll's distinguished career with the Steelers, which had resulted in four Super Bowl championships. This also marked the beginning of NFL free agency, which would alter football and the way things were done.

In the discussion that day, the decision was made that the Steelers would start to draft and select free agents by strongly considering their attitude as part of the process. Don't get me wrong—you cannot win without great athletes, but you surely can also lose with them. If you look at the team that wins the Super Bowl, you will see athletes with big arms, built-up chests, and supernatural speed; but if you take a good look at a team that did not qualify for the playoffs, you will see exactly the same characteristics!

Furthermore, teams have a collective attitude that eventually becomes clear and then becomes that team's culture. Once the culture has formed, inherent strengths and challenges will show up in a pattern of wins and losses.

Shortly after that meeting, the Steelers hired a new head coach, Bill Cowher, who also was very much into attitude—and now was the time to get his input. So when the two of us sat down to talk, I asked him what he thought about bringing in new players. He said he wanted to have players who were able to overcome any sort of adversity—that the "good" players have gone through "something" difficult in their life they were able not only to handle but also to transcend, rising to a higher level of accomplishment.

Chuck Noll, who was Coach Cowher's predecessor, had a saying: "Panic is something you feel when you do not know what you are doing." Cowher, too, wanted to know that his players had confidence even when they faced tough times—to have proof positive from their past that they had confidence even facing adversity.

I personally felt that the ability to trust was a hugely important characteristic in the men recruited and that it translated into their being able to be coached, take instruction, and grow as professionals. Many, if not most of these young athletes, seemed to come from broken families where they had very little contact with a father and were not trusting by nature. Many people believe that trust is an issue in every relationship, but trust, or the unwillingness to trust, is actually an attitude that is shaped from early interactions. An untrusting attitude leaves athletes unconsciously hunting for something to happen to make this attitude "right." They then bring this predominantly untrusting attitude to the game and to life. I believe what Abraham Lincoln said is true: "It is better to trust all the time and sometimes be disappointed than to trust none of the time and be miserable." I would just add four words to the quote: "It is better to trust all the time...than to trust none of the time and be miserable *and be a failure.*" Teammates must trust each other to perform at their peak at all times.

> *Teammates must trust each other to*
> *perform at their peak at all times.*

From those early conversations with the Steelers, I developed interview techniques and tests that looked at internal concepts of individuals, realizing that all people have a way they view the world. They have their own set of "eyes" from which they view everything, and success and happiness are the byproducts of those eyes. Furthermore, those eyes have compartments. In other words, there are different ways we see ourselves—in a family setting, spiritual setting, physical setting, and so forth, and we become that vision in each of those settings. Since then I have gone on to work with teams that have had some success: the University of Miami football team (headlined in a cover story in *Sports Illustrated* that showed how the team evolved from one where people said the school should discontinue playing football to a team with a 30-game-plus winning streak and two National Championships), the Rutgers football team (which went from never playing in a bowl game to participating in four straight), the LSU football team (which won the National Championship), and the Alabama football team (whose surprisingly quick rise in one year made it a contender for the National Championship).

Your happiness or success will, in a sense, "happen before it happens"—first in the mind and then in the real world.

Going for what we want in our own lives is very similar: We want success or happiness, perhaps without knowing these two things are simply byproducts of the way our minds are arranged. If we can identify the way we think and practice thinking differently, then the things we want will in many instances show up. Just like an athlete, you will not be a success if you do not have the specific skills you need within your field of endeavor—and with faulty ways of thinking, you definitely can be a failure. Your happiness or success will, in a sense, "happen before it happens"—first in the mind and then in the real world.

CHAPTER 1

Growing Up

"Get busy living or get busy dying."

—from the movie Shawshank
Redemption

When my father recently passed away, a little eight-year-old girl named Natalie, who is a friend of my daughter Claire, wrote me a note that said, "Mr. Elko, I do not believe that someone grows up until they lose a parent. I am sorry you had to grow up."

Growing up and maturity seem like simple and similar notions, but they are not the same thing at all. The immature person says to himself or herself, "Life should give in to my demands." The mature person says, "I should give in to the demands of life." I've used the term "give in" here because that's the way immature people relate to life. They want life to change and "give in" to their demands. They believe that life should serve them. It's called entitlement. Mature people, on the other hand, are responsive to the demands of life. They change. They serve life. It is not just all about them.

Life's demands change, the economy changes, our children grow up, we lose parents, we lose jobs, and we have to grow upward or decline downward—we do not stay the same. It's called change.

We have to grow upward or decline downward—we do not stay the same.

When I was a young football player, my coach used to ask me every day when I walked off the field, "Did you get better or worse today?" Back then, I wondered what he was talking about. But like most great lessons, this one hit me later, when I became mature enough to understand that he was asking me to "grow upward" when I was on the field, because I was not staying the same—there is no steady state—so if I was not growing, I was dying.

As far as my coach and I are concerned about the question he asked me, when the student is ready, the teacher will arrive. Now I have learned. And I am changing—and growing.

I was listening to National Public Radio the day that Timothy McVey was executed. When a woman who lost her daughter in the bombing of the Federal Building in Oklahoma City was asked if she had any relief from McVey's execution, she said, "None." When the media asked why not, she answered, "If a poisonous snake bites you, would you run and chase the snake or would you address the wound?" She went on, "I never chased that snake. I addressed the wound. I have no relief at all from his death."

That reaction is called growing up. That woman knew the only way she would spiritually survive what happened was to grow and become different in some way, or she was doomed to suffer endlessly. Some people sit around studying a problem or suffering a situation while others go out confident they will find a way forward. People need to change to grow, and can overcome seemingly insurmountable obstacles in order to live their lives to the fullest.

THERAPY

Researcher Hans Eysenck was a bit of a maverick and loved to present data that made people's jaws drop. Years ago he presented research showing that people who went to therapy—no matter if it was with a psychotherapist, psychologist, or psychiatrist—over the course of a year had a lower recovery rate than people who went to see nobody at all. However, modern-day research does not support that. Research today proves that almost all psychotherapies work *if the client works.*

What is different? Therapies have evolved to be more useful than the sessions of the past, where clients sat around for hours just talking about their problems. Modern therapies involve concrete growth strategies, definite plans, and ways to measure progress. This last idea is really important if you want to improve. No measurement equals no improvement. In football we keep score. We measure a lot of things to make sure we keep improving. I call it coaching.

ECONOMICS

Andy Grove was for years the innovative leader of Intel, the world's dominant computer chip manufacturer. One day when at the top of his "game" he announced to his board, "We are going to completely change what we are doing. We are going to quit making the memory chips for computers we presently make—that has us at the top—and start making a totally different component." Although many on the board thought Grove was crazy, they allowed him to go forward. He did, and Intel quickly became the global leader in making microprocessors for personal computers. Had it stayed in the memory business, Intel may not matter or even exist today. It used to be that national economies changed very little over time, but the future is not what it used to be. The new playing field is global.

The new playing field is global.

There are just two groups of people: those who learn and grow and those who do not. Those who do not grow will suffer—in their relationships, in their pocketbooks, even in their spirit—especially in their spirit. Those who can change—for example, when the economy calls for it, or better yet, *before* the economy calls for it, because they see the necessity for change coming—are the winners. And those who can change creatively and dare to take chances toward growth are going to prosper.

In 2004, Nick Saban left his job as head coach of Louisiana State University to go to the professional ranks—to coach the Miami Dolphins. (He had previously worked in the NFL as an assistant coach for the Cleveland Browns.) He quickly left to return to college-level coaching. He became head coach for the University of Alabama. I asked him after he left the pros to go back to college football, what had happened. He said, "When I was an assistant in professional football for the Cleveland Browns, there was no free agency; you basically drafted a player, and then you were stuck with each other and you worked everything out. Pro football changed so much with free agency, and I could not change with it."

Nick is an exception. Because he is very talented and lucky, he had options and could cope—without changing. But most people do not have options like Nick. We have to find a way to grow, not just cope. Instead of sidestepping uncomfortable things, we need to meet these obstacles to our dreams head on. Coping is not the answer. Get a fresh, new vision of your world and *you* in it: That *is* the answer.

> *Coping is not the answer. Get a fresh, new vision of your world and you in it: That is the answer.*

LESSONS FROM A PENCIL

There is a parable told about a pencil maker who took each pencil aside just before putting it "finished" into a box. He would tell the pencil, "There are five things you need to know before I send you out into the world to be the best you can be. First, you will be able to do many great things, but only if you allow yourself to work with others. Second, you will need to experience some sharpening from time to time, but it will make you better. Third, you can correct a mistake by changing it. Fourth, the most important part of you will always be what's inside. Last, on every surface you cover, you must leave your mark." The pencil understood, promised to remember, and went into the box.

Now change places with the pencil.

This parable of the pencil is used in twelve-step programs to help people recover from addiction. For some, the mere mention of these programs turns them off, but the fact of the matter is that these programs *do* work. And in order to change, you have to work within a specific system with a plan, and keep score. Let's say you are very, very thirsty and you see a big glass of ice water. To get that drink, though, you sit there and you wish for the drink and dream of that refreshment, imagining the water flowing through your lips and quenching your thirst. But you don't make any plan to get up and drink the glass of water. How would that work for you? Wouldn't you still be thirsty?

In order to change, you have to work within a specific system with a plan, and keep score.

There is a movement nowadays that suggests you have only to envision the outcome and you will get it—and, indeed, vision is a significant part of growing. Just wishing for something, however, and then expecting to get it is a naive notion that many folks have bought into. Proponents of this movement have told me, "Kevin, you do not think magically or spiritually enough." However, this movement does not have a process spelled out for people to follow—only the *why*, not the *how*. The *how* is hard. Without consistently working a step-by-step system to track progress and reach goals, the "magical" thinking of this movement is delusional.

One of my favorite fables is about a scorpion and a frog:

> Once upon a time there lived a scorpion and a frog. As the frog sat in the warm sun on the bank of a stream, along came a scorpion who wanted to cross to the other side. So he scuttled up to the frog and asked:

"Please, Mr. Frog, can you carry me across the stream on your back?"

"I could," replied the frog, "but I must refuse as you will probably sting me as I swim across."

"But why would I do that?" asked the scorpion. "If I were to sting you, you would die, and I would drown."

Now, the frog knew a thing or two about scorpions, and how lethal they were. But on the other hand, the scorpion had made a point and the point made sense. So the frog agreed. The scorpion climbed onto his back, and together they set off across the stream. About the time they reached the middle of the crossing, the scorpion stung the frog. Mortally wounded, the frog cried out, "Why did you sting me? It's not in your interests to sting me, because now I will die and you will drown."

"I know," replied the scorpion, as he sank into the stream. "But, you see, I am a scorpion. I have to sting you. It's in my nature."

Just as it is natural for the scorpion to sting the frog, it is natural for man to want to avoid change—because change is uncomfortable, and the human condition loves comfort. Growing upward, especially in the beginning, is uncomfortable. In fact, when we are suffering, if change requires an effort on our part, we'll try to make our suffering more comfortable. We'll even create persuasive self-talk to keep from changing and restore our comfort level. We might say, for example, "My uncle smoked until he was 90, so I will be fine." The fact of the matter is we have to get comfortable with getting uncomfortable—in order to change.

We have to get comfortable with getting uncomfortable—in order to change.

Also, we might keep from changing because of the crisis we have over our self-worth. We mistakenly believe that our personal worth is on a sliding scale dictated by other people's opinions or our own constant self-assessments. But the experience of self-worth can and must be earned. Find something you like to do and get good at it. While you're at it, you will change and grow into a person you like. Self-worth won't be an issue for you anymore.

Just as the seasons change, people need to change to grow—and they must grow to live their lives to the fullest.

CHAPTER 2

You Do Not Have to Carry More Than You Can Hold

"If you understand this you will know peace. Some things are within the power of your control and some things are not."

—*Epititus*

Immediately after 9/11, I was asked to come to New York City to work with Merrill Lynch because the company had an office located in the World Financial Center, a building connected to both World Trade Center buildings. The Merrill Lynch office had two of its financial advisors eating breakfast the morning of 9/11 in a restaurant called Windows on the World, along with a number of their clients. When the planes hit, the advisors called their families and then the office to say goodbye. I've been trained in critical stress debriefing and had been on a few emergencies before, so I was honored to help this company and our country at that horrific time.

When I went to work with the New York office, I was surprised to see many workers with casts on their arms and legs because they were trampled in the street during 9/11. In fact, the buildings were still smoldering. One man I met will forever have an impact on me. He was a security guard in one of the World Trade Center buildings. At first, I did not understand what he was saying to me. He said tearfully that he had stood on the ground floor of one of the buildings in a stairwell as the people came down, yelling at the top of his lungs over and over, "Take your heels off! We will save lives if you take your heels off!" He went on to say that few people listened to his plea to remove their shoes so they could run to where they needed to go.

I have the same plea for you today: Take off what you have on that is keeping you from getting where you are called to go. Most people do not get to where they are destined to go because they are carrying some thing (or things) that keep them from getting there. Mentally, take off all that is not part of your vision and all that is slowing you down, and then your vision will find you.

Take off all that is not part of your
vision and all that is slowing you down,
and then your vision will find you.

Researcher Damian Rotter found that 78 percent of the population is driven by something outside of themselves that for them becomes mental clutter. To become part of the 22 percent who are driven internally by clarity of thought and passion, you first must not let the weeds of negative thought take hold and strangle your vision. The closer to pure the thoughts of your vision are, the greater the likelihood your vision will be realized.

You first must not let the weeds of negative
thought take hold and strangle your vision.

The challenge we face is that all day long we have thoughts counter to the vision in our heads. When we let these counter-thoughts sit there, we are letting undesired "weeds" grow beside our vision, squeezing the nutrients from the brain soil, and eventually choking to death what we desire. Like a disciplined gardener daily pulling unwanted weeds, we must constantly remove the weeds of mental clutter growing from external seeds.

A.J. Muste stood outside the White House lawn during the entire Vietnam War, holding a candle. A reporter said, "You will not change the world by doing this." He replied, "I am not trying to change the world. I am doing this so the world does not change me."

Consider for a moment that there is a principle for precision but not for error; for intelligence but not for ignorance; for health, wealth, and happiness but not for disease, poverty, and depression. If you constantly *impress* in your subconscious mind that which your heart truly desires, then that image is expressed in the "picture screen" of your "daily space." To further this principle, if that image is clear—without mental clutter— what is expressed on the picture screen of your daily space is equally clear. The mental clutter comes from invading thoughts that are completely incongruent with the vision you have for yourself and your life. The difference between the fully alive person and the ordinary person is that the ordinary person has some purposeful thoughts; but for the fully alive person, these purposeful thoughts are *all* he or she has.

There are two types of mental clutter—the first being external mental clutter.

YOUR RIGHT TO BE OFFENDED
(INSTEAD, EASE UP; DO NOT JUDGE)

One morning as I was on my way to the airport, I saw a young lady driving her car, looking in the rear-view mirror, putting on her makeup, and talking on the cell phone. She was driving a Ford Focus. When I got to my talk, I mentioned her, describing all her actions, and said, "That is called irony." I was referring to her apparent ability to focus on many things at once—except on the road. After my talk, a woman came up to me and said, "That is one of the most offensive things I have heard in my life because I drive a Focus." Not exactly sure why she was offended, I thought (but kept it to myself), "You have had an easy life. How will you ever make it? Ease up." We need to have more in our life than walking around, looking for something to file in our "offended folder."

These days, more people are walking around offended than ever before; it's a sign of the times. More television programs and news infotainment shows reinforce our right to be offended and give out information that will offend. Of course, we all need to be mindful of people being offended and playing offense at us so that others do not take advantage of us; but these days, people being offended has gone overboard. It's like using a backhoe to dig a small garden in our backyard. Collectively, people are angry, seemingly with the pervading thinking, "It's my right to stand my ground, or else I'll get consumed." There are dozens of opportunities to be offended in a day. But if you harbor thoughts about being offended, then your eyes are on the alert for more. You call out to the world, "Come offend me," and the world *will* respond. Then, so-called friends enter your life who are even more offended than you, and all of a sudden, you're a member of the Isn't-It-Awful Club, manifesting so much offense that you start feeling good about feeling bad. Instead, put forth this exorbitant amount of wasted energy into your vision for your life.

If you harbor thoughts about being offended,
then your eyes are on the alert for more.

In a previous season of my life, I was in the middle of Pennsylvania conducting a workshop intended to build a number of construction companies into a team, sponsored by the Department of Transportation. At the beginning of the workshop, a woman in the crowd, who obviously was not a member of any construction company, started yelling offensive things to me, such as, "How much did they pay you? How much does it cost to feed you?" This harassment went on for the entire workshop. After we finished, I walked over to her to ask what her problem was. I was definitely offended. She said she was aware that the Department of Transportation was putting on this workshop, and she had asked them many times to install a stoplight at a specific intersection where she lived. The department had not responded, and very recently, her parents were killed in an accident at that intersection. Suddenly, I was no longer offended.

If we squeeze an orange, what comes out of the orange is orange juice—because that's what is inside. People are no different; in fact. If we treat most people we meet like they are hurting, we probably will not miss the mark by much; most people *are* hurting. Rewrite your subconscious agreement with everybody you meet so that you consciously, stubbornly refuse to be offended about anything. You can use all that conserved energy for something grand in *this* season of your life.

THAT WAS AWFUL (INSTEAD, SAVE THE LABEL "AWFUL" FOR THE BIG STUFF)

One morning I went to the bank, and when I came out, I watched as a young man in an older pickup truck drove through a parking space next to my car, ripping off the mirror of my new car. He then turned the corner and traveled up the road, carrying off my mirror. Standing there with my jaw hanging open so far it almost touched my chest, I was "ticked off," to say the least. I was thinking, "That was awful, and I can hardly stand it."

When I got home, I decided to take a jog to work off my "this-is-awful-and-I-can't-stand-it" feeling. As I was putting on my running shoes, my little eight-year-old daughter, Claire, ran to me saying, "There is something wrong with Jared," who is my six-year-old son. In the next room I found Jared on the floor, unresponsive, eyes rolled back in his head, and he appeared to be barely breathing. I assumed that he was choking on something, and I thought, "I have moments only here; I am about to lose my son." I yelled for my wife, who was working out in our little gym area right next to where all this was happening. She ran in, arriving at the same conclusion that he was choking, and screamed, "Oh, my God." She started down his throat with her fingers as I was dialing 911. And then he came out of it.

What happened was that our son was lying on top of a big exercise ball, bouncing up and down. He bounced and bounced until he knocked himself out. (I know—I have issues coming down the road with this little guy.) But he was not choking, and after we called the doctor, we realized he was going to be fine. About an hour and a half passed by, and I decided again to go take my jog. As I walked past my car with the ripped-off mirror that I thought a short period ago was awful, after what I had just gone through, you know what I thought now? You can blow the car up or roll it over a hill; I could not care less. Which time was I telling myself the truth—when I thought it was awful that I lost my mirror, or when I could not care less? This kind of "truth" is whatever you choose it to be. Choose wisely. Choices have consequences.

We are at our best when we have the "truths" in our head aligned with facts.

We are at our best when we have the "truths" in our head aligned with facts. It definitely was not a fact that it was awful I lost my mirror, but for a time, that judgment made it a personal truth. And in my mind—to the noise, to the clutter— the idea was overwhelming. How do you know the difference? How do you know for sure that the change in the economy is awful, or the ending of a job is terrible, or that you should hold onto a dead and awful relationship because what is next after you let it go might be much worse? You cannot hold onto this fear and worrisome projection and at the same time hold a vision in your mind and expect anything to manifest itself except the worry; you are praying for what you do not want, and you are *sure* things are awful. Stop this act of arrogance.

When a man in a mental ward says that he is Elvis Presley, and he says it over and over, after a while he is not making it up: He is Elvis. His "Thank you, thank you very much" eventually sounds convincingly like Elvis as well. Similarly, I saw Dustin Hoffman in an interview after he won an academy award for *Rain Man,* and he seemed a bit weird. He played the part so well, he still looked like he had become that character. If you keep telling yourself that things are awful and terrible over and over and that you have no place in today's abundance, you will eventually play that part; it is a "can't miss" proposition.

If you hold onto fear, then that worrisome, awful vision is clearly and consistently established in your mind, and it will occur—because you have made it so.

Fear is an acronym—False Evidence Appearing Real. And if you hold onto fear, then that worrisome, awful vision is clearly and consistently established in your mind, and it will occur—because *you* have made it so. You will be using the principles taught in this book, only in reverse; it is the law of causality—cause and effect—not coincidence, as most people would like to believe.

CHAPTER 3

Cutting the Internal Mental Clutter

"Only in quiet waters do things mirror themselves undistorted. Only in a quiet mind is adequate perception of the world."

—Hans Margolius

While experiencing rain delays over and over during a Wimbledon tennis tournament, Venus Williams said, "I love the delays. Each time they happen I sit down and clear my mind." Venus eventually won the tournament.

You can clear your mind of both external and internal clutter if you learn to repeat to yourself and meditate on phrases such as the following:

> "Trust."

> "No judgment."

> "There is no *hard* if I bring the best *me*."

> "Pressure is something you feel when you do not know what you are doing, and I know what I am doing."

> "I'm taking my heels off."

In the sections that follow, we consider a few of the kinds of things that can clutter our minds.

THE NEED TO BE LIKED
(INSTEAD, SAY IT'S NICE TO BE LIKED, BUT I DON'T NEED IT)

A great book by Terri Cole Whitaker, titled *What You Think of Me Is None of My Business,* discusses approval addiction. Many people have this addiction, spending their entire day trying to retrieve information that they are liked. They are like CSI techs working overtime looking to collect evidence that the people who matter (and that would be just about everyone) like and think highly of them. This doesn't leave much time to have a life.

Yes, I, too, *want* people to like me; *like* is a wonderful thing, but I don't *need* people to like me. I need water and oxygen, not things I make up. Approval-seeking consumes energy.

Approval-seeking consumes energy.

Metaphorically, if water were self-worth, it would be as if you were walking around holding out a large empty cup to everybody you meet, asking them to pour water into the cup to fill it up. The problem is, there is a hole in that cup; the hole is that everybody must approve of you, and when they do, your self-worth goes up, but when they don't, your "water" oozes out. So, no matter what anybody says positive, you need more and more water, the approval addiction. Patch that hole in the cup by telling *yourself* over and over that you do not need others' approval to have high personal worth; *you* tell yourself you have self-worth. Tell yourself until it sticks, until that hole is "stopped up."

> *You do not need others' approval to have high personal worth; you tell yourself you have self-worth.*

When you trust these internal urges that are screaming at you, you can't live fully. Others may not like it when you do not seek their approval, because they want you to do things for them; their "what can you do for me?" philosophy requires all your energy. If you are powered by needing someone else's approval—often anyone else's—rather than your own, you will surrender your vision for their self-serving one. There may be some who think you are a "vehicle" for them to drive around; say "Enough!" to them. And do not expect them to like your changed behavior or to like *you*—because they really didn't like you anyway; they just liked what you *did* for them, and of course they want you to continue. If you are going to make others' opinion of you be your everything, you will never get to your life, your vision.

Comedian Bill Cosby once said, "I don't know the key to success, but the key to failure is trying to please everybody." If you are a parent and have the vision that your children will be self-disciplined individuals who understand the importance of serving and giving to others, and then you clutter that vision because you need their approval, now you are not the parent but rather nothing more than another friend. Therefore, when the time comes to stand up to teach your children the kinds of things that align with a life vision, and you instead give in to your need to be liked, how will your children turn out? Or let's say you are an executive with a grand vision that a number of people are dependent on, but you have an employee or a group of employees who are sabotaging the entire picture—and you have a need for their approval. How do you think that will work for you?

Your self-worth does not change with others' opinions of you. Indeed, living in this way does not mean you always like *what* you do, so you will have to *change your behavior* from time to time. However, you have to like *who* you are. Free yourself by following what is *inside* of you, not what is outside of you—the opinion of others. Use this energy more wisely. Let this mental clutter go: You'll have one less thought interfering with your grand vision, and large amounts of energy will be released.

EXPECTING TOO HARD AND NOT BRINGING THE BEST YOU TO EVERY EVENT

When I was working with the University of Miami football program, we played a National Championship game against the University of Nebraska. At the time we had a player who won the Academic Heisman Trophy playing offensive tackle, Joaquin Gonzalez.

I spoke to the team before the game, and then I threw a football to Joaquin, asking him to talk to the team about what they needed to do to win against Nebraska. He said, "I expect this game against Nebraska to be a tough game and I expect the player across from me to be a great player. So I plan on bringing the best *me* every play, and I will refuse to take any plays off." That game was not very hard, because the team listened to him and expected hard, which made winning easy.

When you have a feeling that something is too hard, that feeling is simply a warning signal that you are to bring the best you. The mistake occurs when you *judge* something as too hard; such judgments stop miraculous things from happening. If you avoid judging the event, stay on the path of your vision, and use a great word that you can repeat to yourself during these times (such as *trust*), you will gain the momentum for victory. Say, "I *trust* that I will learn what I need to overcome," "I *trust* that I will end up where I am supposed to be as long as I stay disciplined and on my path," and "I *trust* that the vision will arrive if I stay away from judgment of events." *Trust.*

When you judge something as too hard,
such judgments stop
miraculous things from happening.

Have you ever heard a story about a young child trapped underneath a car and the mother picking the car up? That feat defies physics, yet there are numerous reports of this kind of event happening. How did this miracle happen? And would it have happened if the mother had the thought, "This is too hard and cannot be done"?

When people are interviewed about looking back over their lives and whether they have any regrets, many have said, "Yes." But eight out of ten regrets were *not* that they failed at something but rather that they had an urge to do something and did not. Furthermore, most did not try because they judged the task to be too hard. If you ever meet someone who has achieved what you did not try, I guarantee you'll think, "If that person has done it, I surely could have." That is regret.

When I was doing a seminar at The Broadmoor in Colorado Springs, a man walked up to me and said, "You saved my life." I asked, "How did I do that?" He said he was diagnosed with a disease called PAN at Johns Hopkins University and was given six months to live; this diagnosis happened five years ago. On that same day, two other young men his age were diagnosed, and they died within six months. He said that after he was diagnosed, he put on one of my CDs and in it I said, "Don't quit." I asked him, "Did I say more than that?" I had a lot of education and information on the disc. He said, "No, that was all I heard you say." He went on to tell me he needed to hear this because he had a wife and a beautiful daughter, so he decided not to quit, even though he felt like it. He added, "Thanks for saving my life."

Know what you are doing, and keep doing it and trust that you are prepared to receive.

Steelers head coach Chuck Noll used to say, "Pressure is something you feel when you do not know what you are doing." Know what you are doing, and keep doing it and trust that you are prepared to receive. Then when you are supposed to, you *will* receive, especially during challenging times. *Trust.*

The University of Miami was playing Ohio State for the National Championship in the Fiesta Bowl one year and the Miami kicker, Todd Sievers, had to make a last-second field goal to tie the game and take it into overtime. Ohio State called time out a number of times to get Todd to think about the kick, to freeze him. So when he walked over by me, I just kept repeating over and over to him, "Trust." He went out and put the ball through the uprights. Trust can reduce mental clutter, give focus, and provide confidence.

Trust can reduce mental clutter, give focus, and provide confidence.

NOT FORGIVING—
THE ULTIMATE MIND CLUTTER

An organization called the Million Dollar Round Table once gave me an opportunity to speak, and they had a woman at the event whose photograph as a child you've probably seen before: She was the little girl running with her back on fire out of a village that was exploding with napalm during the Vietnam War. She has since left Vietnam, and her vision now in this season of her life is to help children who have been hurt by war. She is a powerful speaker and a giant spirit. She was invited to attend an event at the Vietnam Memorial in Washington, D.C. There, a man came up to her to tell her he was the captain who gave the order to fire on her village—to bomb it. He was told that the village was empty, so he ordered the bombing. The man went on to tell her that his life did not seem to work.

She said to this man, who approached her now-healed wounds, to go heal his own; he was and had been forgiven. Presently this man has a life, family, and a career that works: He is a Methodist minister. As you can predict, this woman's life also really works: She has raised a fortune for kids, and her life is filled with joy because she allowed the grand picture to manifest itself.

Holding resentment is like taking poison and expecting someone else to get sick. You must learn to forgive. Forgiving does not mean you are giving someone who has hurt you power over you. Instead, by forgiving, you are no longer attached to what has occurred, so the one who is going free is you. Imagine the energy consumed and the ice water thrown on the positive pictures ready to manifest in your head when you walk around contemplating an injury someone did to you in the past—and how much worse if you harbor these bad feelings for any period of time. Nothing will shut down where you are going faster than not forgiving. In fact, your grand vision will not arrive when you are sitting around holding on to upset.

*By forgiving, you are no longer
attached to what has occurred, so
the one who is going free is you.*

As comedian Buddy Hackett once put it, while you are at home holding a grudge against someone, that person is out dancing, so who is really suffering here?

My forgiveness strategy is quite simple: If something happens to me, I close my eyes and meditate on the thought "Bring that person peace." If that does not work and I continue to hold on to the grudge, I send that person a gift. Here is why: You do not attract what you *want* but instead attract what you *are*. If you are walking around bitter, then guess what you are attracting—bitterness. Forgiveness is a powerful strategy that opens the door to allow positive energy to flow to you. Bring yourself peace.

*Forgiveness is a powerful strategy
that opens the door to allow
positive energy to flow to you.*

Clutter is everywhere, and in today's chaotic world you'll see more of it than ever, which will challenge any vision you have. Instead, just focus...and trust.

CHAPTER 4

Just One Last Play

*"Man cannot discover new oceans
unless he has the courage to
lose sight of the shore."*

—Andre Gide

When I was working for the Dallas Cowboys, we had a big game against our arch rivals, the Washington Redskins. During the week-long buildup before the game, Redskins player Albert Connell, in an ESPN interview, made some cutting comments about Deion Sanders, saying that he was an old man who was washed up and should no longer be playing.

In the game, while Deion was trying to disprove these remarks, he caught a punt early in the first quarter and was immediately hit by a number of Redskins. They hit him so hard that Deion suffered such a concussion that the medical staff had to help him off the field. At least for that day, it *did* look like Deion was done. He stayed on the sideline for most of the rest of the game with an ice pack on his spinal cord.

Throughout the game, Deion pleaded with the staff to let him back in. But they said the results could be catastrophic. Later, the stand-in Cowboy punt returner, Jeff Ogden, went onto the field in place of the injured Sanders to receive a punt. Deion suddenly sprinted out, physically removed Ogden's helmet, put it on himself, and ordered Ogden off the field. The doctors were screaming, "Call time out; he's going to kill himself!" But it was too late. Deion caught that punt, broke into a run up the sideline, stiff-armed a player, juked past another, and sprinted into the end zone for a touchdown.

Still it wasn't over. Deion walked to the Redskins sideline. "Hey, Connell," he said, "It isn't any fun hunting rabbits when the rabbit has a gun, too." Then he went to the Dallas sideline, returned Ogden's helmet, and proceeded to the locker room to shower.

What if you had just one play in you, one opportunity? What would it be? Think about it in light of your career, your health, your family and friends. Here is your starting point. Say to yourself, "I have one shot, one season, and this is the way I will manage it. My time has come. I'm making my plan to grow, getting my vision clear—now."

> *What if you had just one play in you, one opportunity? What would it be?*

MAKE THE LAST PLAY COUNT

Paul "Bear" Bryant, the legendary head football coach of the University of Alabama, knew the value of thinking about the last play, and demonstrated that when doing a television commercial for AT&T the week before Mother's Day. As he settled into the studio, those doing the filming said the ad would be easy. They told him just to read the script they held next to the camera, so they practiced while he read, "This is Paul Bryant, the head coach of Alabama, and this weekend is Mother's Day. Call your mama."

The Bear told the studio staff he was ready and that he didn't need a script. Uneasy, the producers decided to go ahead and try it. The Bear said, "This is Paul Bear Bryant, the head coach of the University of Alabama. Roll, Tide, roll," he began. "This weekend is Mother's Day; call your mama," he said. But then he added one more line of his own: "I wish I could...."

Think as if every play is your last and seize your moments.

I'm talking about thinking as if every play is your last and seizing your moments. Sometimes they are as dramatic as The Bear's, but there are many, and their lengths vary: the high-school season; then, the four-years-in-college season; the dating season; the starting-out-on-your-own season; the just-married season; and on and on. Each season of your life calls you to make something of it. After each season, you do not want to say, "Why didn't I enjoy that more, give it more, be in less of a hurry? There was something I was called to do there, and I missed it."

Why not ask, "What are my gifts? What makes me feel alive? Where will my opportunities lead me?" If you feel it is your season to become rich, then ask yourself, "What is rich?" Is it more money so you can bless others with your wealth? Is rich being a better father, mother, or friend? Does being rich mean you reach the top spot in your field? Figure out the answer to this question and others in the same vein concerning your vision during your "preseason." This is a time to try out new ideas and new ways of showing up before the next season—or chapter—of your life gets into full swing.

Each season of your life calls you to make something of it.

LET YOUR LIGHT SHINE

Maybe your last play comes to you as a gift that only you can give. Then grab that gift.

Since coach Butch Davis has been at the University of North Carolina, I have spoken to the team every month, starting with an excerpt from Nelson Mandela's inaugural speech: "Our deepest fear is not that we are inadequate. Our deepest fear is that we are powerful beyond measure. It is our light, not our darkness, that most frightens us. Our playing small does not serve the world. There is nothing enlightened about shrinking so other people do not feel insecure around us. We were all made to shine as children do. It is not just in some of us. It is in everyone. And as we let our own light shine, we unconsciously give others permission to do the same. As we are liberated from our own fear, our presence automatically liberates others." Then, the entire team stands and sings a simple song: "This little light of mine, I'm gonna let it shine; these are my brothers here, I'm gonna help them shine."

That's all there is: Shine your light, and in the process, help others shine theirs. That's how you make that play count. Do your work, make your play, give your donation, and help others give theirs. This shining is showing off your personal gift. There's nothing wrong with shining. However, people do sometimes make mistakes in two different ways when assessing their personal gifts: (1) they think they have no gifts, or (2) they think they have many. The fact is we all have at least one, and sometimes maybe two. But we must quit wasting time developing too many gifts—or worse, wasting time developing none. Find that one definitive special gift, work it into your vision, develop your plan, and grow it in its season to shine. And shine as brightly as you can.

> *Find that one definitive special gift, work it into your vision, develop your plan, and grow it in its season to shine.*

MAKE A GOOD CHOICE WITH YOUR LAST PLAY OF A SEASON

A woman stood alongside a river, carrying a sack. Walking by her, a very hungry man asked if she had any food. "Yes," she said and opened the sack. When she did, the man spotted a precious stone inside and he asked her if he could have the stone instead. "Certainly," she said and easily gave it to him. He walked away, thinking, "I will never be hungry again. This stone is worth the kind of money that will allow me to eat for the rest of my life." But then, he turned around and returned the stone to the woman. He said, "I do not want the stone. I want what is in you that enabled you to give me that stone."

The precious secret, just like the one this woman had, starts inside—and you find it by realizing what you love to spend your time with. Match that love with your one gift you are developing, the thing you do better than anything else, and then time is irrelevant; it just flies by. Time flying means you are in your "sweet spot." Match those two things—love and your gift with your time— and you bring out your best. Get your thoughts, actions and spoken words aligned and congruent to bring out of you in that season what is in you, not only to do more, but to be more and to bring to you what you now deserve.

SECURITY

A lot of people hesitate when it comes to grabbing life as if every play were their last. To leap seems risky, and they want security.

Recently a long-time friend called me, complaining of a sleeping problem. He also told me that he was soon acquiring a company of which he would be its president. He planned to pay for the company at a rate of ten percent a year for ten years; after that time he would own it outright. He said that he and his family needed security, and that would be his sole focus for the next ten years. He confessed that something in the plan was keeping him up at night; I asked if he loved what he was doing. Silence ensued for about ten seconds. I don't remember his response because the long pause *was* the answer.

My friend believes he is secure with this plan, but he can't sleep, and chances are his health will soon deteriorate. If he follows this path, he may not even be around to *see* the future he's sacrificing himself for. Helen Keller once said, "Life is either a daring adventure or nothing. Security does not exist in nature, nor do the children of men as a whole experience it. Avoiding danger is no safer in the long run than outright exposure." Security, especially today, is a myth. You must do what you love; if your body is telling you something is not working, know that you need to rethink your vision. That may involve risk, but think of it as your last play.

You must do what you love; if your body is telling you something is not working, know that you need to rethink your vision.

Playwright August Wilson wrote about three men working in a grocery store before Thanksgiving. They are all promised hams, which they never receive. One man chants the entire play, "I want my ham." The second man says to the third, "He's crazy! That's all he chants all day." The third replies, "Maybe we are not crazy enough. Maybe we became sane and settled for what we did not get, but he refused to settle; in some cases sanity is overrated. He wanted more and he wanted what he deserved."

If you risk and want more than what is safe, others often think something is "wrong" with you. But do not settle for safe. Listen, risk, match your gifts with what makes you feel alive, and then win, hands down. Act as if each moment is the last play.

Do not settle for safe. Listen, risk, match your gifts with what makes you feel alive

---

CHAPTER 5

Seasons of Life

*"To every thing there is a season,
and a time to every purpose
under the heaven."*

—*Ecclesiastes 3:1,* King James Bible

Once, when I was working with a financial company, the CEO had us all in a meeting to tell us he was upset that his sales team gave a great performance until the middle of July, when they all quit performing. He couldn't explain it. I asked him if he had a built-in "season" like a competitor we both knew, and he replied, "No." I told him that meant his sales team had built in its own season, because they needed rest in the middle of July.

People must change and grow upward within a series of seasons. Growth progresses through cycles.

People must change and grow upward within a series of seasons. Growth progresses through cycles.

As I work with Corporate America, I watch teams roll out a product, attempt to sell it, install it, serve it, and at the end of a given time the team measures the results, *rests,* and then starts up a different project to begin the cycle of achievement all over again. I have found that when businesspeople complete this total cycle and then start over again, they work well together—at least much better than if they did not have "seasons" for their task. They have a higher morale and are more excited. Moreover, they are productive. They may not consciously realize they are respecting the seasons of life. But they are, and it works for them. It will work for you, too.

For years it's been said that diets don't work. People's weight see-saws, and those who lose weight gain the weight back. We all have a friend, or know a friend of a friend, who seems to be trapped in this miserable spiral.

Consider, though, that maybe diets *do* work. A diet is nothing more than the dieter's "eating" season. During that season the dieter—with a picture of how he or she is going to look and a plan to get there—places skinny pictures all over the house as a reminder of the plan and the process, then executes the plan. But when the dieter gets to the "rest" period and "lets go" for a bit, then he or she labels himself or herself as a loser. Next, the flood gates (or I should say the "food gates") open, signaling futility and failure. What the dieter needs to do instead of quitting is to begin another eating season.

Think "season" and think "project," because we appear to be designed that way. Nature has seasons, and so do our lives. We have seasons during which we change and grow. We have seasons of rest. When we are intentionally in each season, we grow and prosper and enjoy. Without our intent, seasons will come and go on their own, and probably not to our great benefit.

PREPARATION—THE PRESEASON

Two days after the launch of Apollo 13, an electrical fault caused an explosion in a Service Module oxygen tank, resulting in a complete loss of oxygen and electrical power. A radio transmission from James Lovell lives famously on: "Houston, we have a problem." Despite great hardship caused by severely limited power, cabin heat, and water, the crew successfully returned to Earth. In an interview after the crew landed safely, Lovell was asked how he could be so cool and how the crew members were able to overcome what appeared to be a catastrophic failure. Lovell said that the flight crew had intensively prepared for the unexpected to happen. When asked if they prepared for the specific "problem," he said they did not. But the season of disciplined preparation for the unexpected allowed them to go into a problem-solving mode and be successful, as opposed to a panic mode and not be successful.

The preseason is the time when two things become clear: (1) what exactly you want to happen, and (2) how you are going to do it.

The preseason is the time when two things become clear: (1) what exactly you want to happen, and (2) how you are going to do it. When one team can upset a much better team, there is almost always a definable reason: Maybe the superior team did not take the other team seriously during preparation week. So they arrive unprepared. The unprepared team will likely "wake up" during the game, realizing that a game is won or lost during the week before it is played. But the realization will be too little too late.

By the time the players get to the field, their play should be all "muscle memory," what they have encoded through repetition during the week, so that the win is basically subliminal. For this exact reason, you need the preseason. It's a contemplative time period to map out what you want to become, how you are going to grow, what obstacles may present themselves, and how you will overcome those obstacles—the steps to realize your vision.

When I worked with the Louisiana State University team that won the National Championship, every player said that the "start" happened when they got together and dreamed about the journey to the National Championship and the end result. The dream happened months before it happened, in the preseason, with much careful work—exercising, planning special plays, learning about each other as a team, growing as a family.

> *If you don't dream first, the higher place will never happen.*

Many people try to jump into changing and growing without dreaming first. If you don't dream first, the higher place will never happen. But this step involves a little bit more. The preseason helps you get ready for action, not just by getting a vision about what area to grow in, but all the specific ways to enact this growth—through careful thought, discussion, prayer, sleeping on the dream, and writing it down.

ACTION—THE SEASON

A man had a wife who was losing her battle with cancer. One day he got the courage to ask her, "How does it feel to know that you are dying?" Her reply was swift and timeless: "How does it feel pretending you are not?"

You are probably not dying and, in fact, might be in the best shape of your life. You may be a healthy, young football player in your freshman year of college, or a young financial advisor, looking ahead to her bright future. But the reality we all face is that *this* season of your life will change. What your life is about right now will likely not last forever. If you do not do something with this season of your life that you are now enjoying, then life will march on and an opportunity will be lost.

What your life is about right now will likely not last forever.

During the season, you must consistently keep your vision clear, because at this point things can start getting foggy. Maybe there is a failure or someone "fumbles" the ball. You can get tired, and then in comes mental clutter—thoughts and internal pictures that differ from your vision. Keep to the plan and follow the process in order to grow in your season. If your goal is for a healthy body, this is the time when you are drinking the designated amount of water each day, eliminating snacking by reaching for the water bottle every time you have the urge, walking 20 minutes a day, and so on. This is the time of *doing*, and at first, there is resistance, but you have to get small wins here. You need to want what you want; get up and go for it. And always measure your progress. If you don't, you won't.

Keep to the plan and follow the process in order to grow in your season.

THE BYE WEEK

In a football season there are bye weeks, baseball and basketball an all-star break. This is a time when a team does not play but instead recuperates, rests. This is not the end of the season; instead, the team just slows down. A bye week for you may be Christmas or Hanukkah; you are slowing down to take a few days off to "recharge." However, don't let this break spiral into an off-season but rather recognize the downtime for what it is. Use it, regroup, and refocus your plan.

MAINTAIN AND ACCELERATE— THE PLAYOFFS

At the 1998 Olympic Games in Japan, the U.S. hockey team was the favorite to win the gold medal but instead the Czech Republic won it. Jaromír Jágr, who led the Czech Republic's team to the gold, wears the number 68 when he plays because 1968 was the year of the Russian occupation of Czechoslovakia. At the 1998 Olympics the Czech team beat Canada for the gold medal.

But first, they had to play Russia. Before the game Jágr stood up and said to the rest of the team, "I dedicate this game to my grandfather and anyone else who lost their life during the occupation."

Some people during this "high-energy" season— the playoffs—say, "I cannot do this," a thought which at this point sabotages everything. Others may say, "I've got this whipped," also a defeatist attitude, insomuch as it is disrespectful of the challenge, and will consequently sabotage everything as well. This is the time to stayed focused, "claim the prize," and finish strong. It comes when the end is near, when rest is near, when the time to sit and reevaluate before you begin a new cycle of seasons. You can push and hang on because rest is around the corner. Here you must stay awake to danger signs that make you want to "quit early," and overconfidence may surface as a mindset of defeat. Every player needs a 68—and so do you.

This is the time to stayed focused, "claim the prize," and finish strong.

REST—THE OFF-SEASON

I have been with a number of teams that have
done well, and only a few that have not. One
team I worked with that did not do well was the
Cleveland Browns. One reason is that the person
who ran the team, one of my best friends, was not
able to rest—he was always on the go; it is his
strength. An overplayed strength, however, can
become a weakness. The Sabbath for NFL players is Tuesday; it's the day when the players get
away to relax because they play on Sundays, are
preparing on Saturdays, and are usually traveling
on Mondays or in physical therapy. Tuesday is a
day of rest. However, my friend could not accept
that players needed a rest day, so he would schedule them to voluntarily do things—like see me.
They never got a "break," so I was not very effective because the players were not really "present"
when they came to see me. My friend did not
know about seasons, so the team suffered.

> *Many problems arise from people's inability to "just sit there" and take a "time out."*

Many problems arise from people's inability to "just sit there" and take a "time out." Physical illness, lack of productivity, anger, and panic attacks can often be related to one's inability to rest. Personally, every time I catch myself not being who I would like to be, it's because I am having a problem with rest. Perhaps I did not get time to laugh and play with my family, or I did not get an opportunity just to talk to a friend. Once again we are talking about being in tune with seasons of our own life. And of course we need to develop an awareness of the seasonal needs of other people.

CHAPTER 6

The Preseason: It Happens Before It Happens

"A vision is not just a picture of what could be; it is an appeal to our better selves, a call to become something more."

—Rosabeth Moss Canter

One Saturday afternoon I received a call that my father was very quickly passing from this life. Jumping into my car, I drove an hour to see him, and when I pulled up, my younger sister parked beside me. She put her arm in mine and we walked in together. My sister kneeled down at our father's bed, cradled him in her arms, and told him to go feel peace and joy now. He took his last breath and exhaled it on her cheek. After my mother and older sister offered a gently loving farewell, I kneeled down and told my buddy goodbye. Then we hugged one another as a family, and my younger sister started to talk.

She noted that my father died on his birthday, March 28, and that this funeral was going to be a celebration of his life. She said she had a vision of us all coming together, giving my father the kind of celebration he would love and deserve. For the next couple days, we talked about what we were going to do with the service as a whole, then what each of us was going to do individually, and then how the celebration itself should go. And we followed through with this vision.

My father was a fireman and Freemason, so we had countless firemen and his lodge brothers at the funeral home, performing touching ceremonies and giving tribute about what my father had meant to them. In the funeral procession, we had fire trucks blowing their sirens. Because my father was also a Marine, at the cemetery Marines lined the path from the hearse to the gravesite, giving him a 21-gun salute. Following the service, two soldiers folded an American flag and kneeled down to hand it to my mother.

We all live in circumstance or vision.

My sister had moved us from circumstance, a loss of a loved one, to vision, the season of celebration. We all live in circumstance or vision. This event was clearly a celebration that happened because of vision, and it happened before it happened as a result of my sister starting the vision.

When I was working for the Cleveland Browns, the team went into the playoffs and had a first-round game against the Pittsburgh Steelers. In the game the Brown's starting quarterback, Kelly Holcomb, was on fire. He had more than 400 yards passing against a very good playoff team and may have had over 500 yards passing if a player had not dropped a pass right at the end of the game. This kind of game is more than special. Going over to him, I asked how he did it, and he said, "I played the entire game on Tuesday. Everything that happened on the field today, every catch, touchdown, first down, you name it, I already saw it and played it over and over in my head long before I walked on the field."

That day he was focused on one thing: opportunity. He had his mind on alert, blocking out all else, directing his eyes to find opportunity. He was programmed by his vision. What you get is what you see.

Nelson Mandela is a man who was able to change the world because he lived from his imagination, not his past. In prison those twenty-some years, even though his jailors were giving him scraps of bread and a bucket of water a day for his sustenance, he didn't come out cold and bitter into the world. Instead, he came out focused on the future and living in peace, concentrating on a world free from apartheid, furthering his life's work and vision, not the past. He concentrated on the positive.

Whatever we concentrate on increases.
If we concentrate on beginnings without
judgment or limitations,
we can create miracles.

Whatever we concentrate on increases. If we concentrate on awful, terrible, and endings, we produce awful, terrible, and endings. If we concentrate on beginnings without judgment or limitations, we can create miracles. Living in our vision doesn't eliminate problems, but it *does* strip problems of their authority, supplying within them the crumbs of opportunity that can manifest into a "prosperity banquet."

These crumbs grow in one way: using your imagination. However, many people say to themselves, "Imagination? Isn't that genetic?" No, imagination is a muscle you must use. Watch children: They all have imagination, but often as they age, they stop using it, and so their imagination shrivels up. Use your imagination to concentrate on making something great happen—before it happens.

AGAINST THE ODDS

When I was a child and "misbehaved," I was disciplined by having to go visit my grandmother, who lived a few blocks away. It felt like I spent my youth with her. She had a way of setting me straight that has been a gift that keeps on giving. One morning I woke up to the sound of my father crying in the kitchen. He was a Marine, and Marines do not cry. So I walked out to the kitchen to ask what was going on; he said my grandmother was diagnosed with an aggressive form of leukemia and had fewer than ten days to live.

I went to see her. She was playing the piano, singing hymns, when I walked in. I said, "Dad said you are going to die." She asked, "Does it look like that's what I am sitting here doing? Who told him that?" I answered, "The doctors." She said, "Go back home and tell him the doctors are not God. I have things to do, and I will go when I am ready." She lived, not days, not months, but years longer.

I have heard of patients being told they have a year to live and they died within a few days because they thought their life was over. I have heard of patients being told they have a few days to live and, not believing it, they lived for many years. Much research says the very way we view something, such as an event, a job, or the future, *does* change that which we are viewing. If you can see the opportunity, then opportunity is on its way. All great things are imagined and believed long before they happen, even when there's not one bit of evidence that the person with the vision in the end-of-the-road situation can climb out of his or her hole. Yet that person calmly adheres to what some would label as a "crazy belief." This much-talked about "leap of faith" underlies so many who have achieved the extraordinary. No vision or obstacle is too great to embrace or overcome.

The very way we view something, such as an event, a job, or the future, does change that which we are viewing.

The Australian yachting team was truly "down under" in 1983 when it came to the America's Cup; they were in last place. Interestingly, part of their preparation for the race was to pair up to listen to a recording of an announcer broadcasting an imaginary race of the Australians winning the America's Cup, three times a day for four years—or 5,000 times. They came to Rhode Island and went from being the worst team to the best team (first place) and won the America's Cup. The trophy had remained in the hands of the New York Yacht Club for well over a century—and the 1983 win by the Australians ended the longest winning streak in the history of sport. When their leader was asked about their transformation and remarkable win, he said, "No, what is the big deal? We already won it 5,000 times and now it is 5,001."

If you imagine winning a race again and again, then your mind is instructing your eyes concerning what to look for to win the race. If you imagine being an unbelievably great husband, wife, parent, and so on, your mind tells your hands and feet to act accordingly. The mind achieves not only what it conceives and believes, but it also advises the senses. Life will live up to the thoughts and images you have about it, so why not imagine a spectacular future? However, you must do it over and over. And the repeated image must be of one thing, not many contrasting things. The more embedded the vision, the more it flourishes.

The repeated image must be of one thing, not many contrasting things.

THE FOUR LEGS OF A CHAIR

If you have ever watched a lion tamer go into a lion's cage, you've noticed that he usually has a stun gun, a whip, and a chair with four legs. So what in the world will a chair with four legs do to stop a lion? In actuality, when a lion looks at four different things at one time, it is paralyzed; it does not know what to react to, so it reacts to nothing.

Our imagination and visualization work the same way. We sit and visualize opportunity in our lives for a period of time, maybe even for some time each day. But then, we walk around the rest of the day, worrying and thinking about what we do not want. By worrying you are actually praying for what you do not want, sending a signal that you have on your mind those catastrophic things and giving them a chance to manifest.

> *By worrying you are actually*
> *praying for what you do not want.*

Norman Cousins wrote a story that once during a football game a first-aid station treated five people for suspected food poisoning. It was discovered the five had bought drinks from a particular refreshment stand. An announcement went over the loud speaker not to buy drinks from this particular stand because of the possibility of food poisoning. Before long, more than 200 people complained of food poisoning symptoms. Nearly half of the symptoms were so severe that they were taken to the hospital.

After a little more investigative work, however, it was discovered that the original five had eaten tainted potato salad from a particular deli on the way to the game. When the other "ill" people found out that their drinks from the stadium were safe, they experienced a recovery that could be rivaled only by Lazarus.

Most do not realize how powerful the mind is. But yet, the mind cannot truly discern between what is real and what is imagined, so we can use this property of the mind. If you imagine over and over that you are a champion, the mind believes in that reality and acts accordingly. As St. Augustine said, "Faith is believing what you do not see; the reward of faith is to see what you believe." Keep positive, not negative, and reap the notable benefits.

THE WHEEL OF FORTUNE

"The Wheel of Fortune" is a powerful metaphor for living. The Wheel of Fortune is a concept from medieval and ancient philosophy referring to the capricious nature of Fate. The wheel belongs to the goddess Fortuna, who spins it at random, changing the positions of those on the wheel—some suffer great misfortune, whereas others gain windfalls. The term lives on today through the *Wheel of Fortune* game show, where contestants win or lose prizes on a random spin of the wheel. Many people constantly live in circumstance, dealing with the ups and downs of the day. Abraham Maslow said that most people are overdeveloped survivors and underdeveloped achievers. If something good happens, which they are often not even responsible for, they feel good; but if something bad happens, then we know how they feel—endlessly riding up and down the Wheel throughout their days. Life is something that happens to them throughout the seasons.

At the center of the Wheel is the hub, that place where you live when you have a vision. In the hub, security is not your bank account, job, investments, spouse, or your recent checkup. It is your ability to connect with your vision, with something larger, and to create what you are called to create. At the hub is your ability to still your mind and direct it simply to that which brings you peace and joy.

> *At the hub is your ability to still your mind and direct it simply to that which brings you peace and joy.*

How do you know if you are in the hub or if you are on the rim? The people out on the rim are always running a race, but they are not sure where or how it ends. Their focus is on scarcity, so they are always looking to what they have, what they do not have, and what others have. They think there are only so many "pieces of the pie," so they have to get their slice—and it needs to be bigger than everybody else's piece. It *appears* this is a group of achievers, but it is really a group of mediocrity.

Often this group suffers from "hurry" sickness, anxiety, or some other stress disorder. This group lacks rest and is motivated by worry as well as by what is theirs and what is not yet theirs.

The people in the center of the hub are very different because they live in their vision—they believe in abundance, in unlimited pieces of pie. Theirs can be large or small—however they like it and according to what matters for them. You know you are in the hub when your visualization has noble intentions; and when the visualization is acted out, it gives you peace and joy. Here you are not driven to endlessly compete.

One day at the Dallas Cowboys training complex, when I was getting ready to talk to the team, a backup running back named Troy Hambrick came up to me and said, "Doc, I hated hearing you speak before, but I love hearing you now." I ask him why he loved me now, and he said, "Emmitt Smith told me that I love you." (I thought to myself that I wish I knew Emmitt when I was single.)

I then went up to Emmitt Smith to ask him what he said to Troy. He said he told Troy he wanted him to listen to me because he wanted him to get better at his position. I then asked Emmitt why, given that Troy was his backup and that he was competing with Troy. Emmitt said he did not compete. Rather, he had created a vision for himself and hoped that others, including his backup, had the same vision. He said he believed in abundance and that there was "enough" to go around.

Emmitt was living, dreaming, and manifesting in the hub. He's a prime example of growth motivation, as he taught his sport of football living from the hub. In his world, life was overflowing with the fullness of possibilities and prosperity.

RADIO WAVES

Linda Hundt, who started Sweetie-licious Pie Pantry in DeWitt, Michigan, is one of the most alive people I have ever met. Leaving her home each day intentional in her internal imagery, Linda tells herself she will touch someone— someone who will walk into her shop—and be a blessing to that person that day. That is what "rich" means to her in this season of her life.

The end of summer is rhubarb season, and each year, on a specific day, Linda cooks a rhubarb custard pie (not your everyday pie) for an elderly couple she knows. This particular day, she left the house thinking she was going to be a blessing to this couple, sending out "radio waves" as I like to call them. (You could simply call them "vibes.") However, the vendor who delivers her rhubarb did not show up. So she called her husband (who also grows rhubarb) and asked him to leave work, go home, pick his rhubarb, and bring it to her. He did, and she even had extra rhubarb, so she cooked two pies. Just as she finished, a distraught woman walked into Linda's shop with her elderly mother and asked Linda to help her; she was on her way to visit her brother and had gotten lost. Linda said, "Sure, I'll help you. Sit down. I am going to give you and your mother some quiche while we get you directions."

As she ate, the lost lady went on to tell Linda that she had not been to Michigan for 40 years and that she and her mother were driving to Flint to spend some time with her dying brother. Then she said, "By the way, I know this is a crazy and impossible request, because we already looked everywhere for it, but my brother has been asking us for a pie he ate when he was a kid, and since we are here, do you know where we could find him a rhubarb custard pie?" Linda responded, "I just happen to have an extra, fresh-baked one for you here today. The angels are definitely on your side."

Many of the prosperity books that are popular today state this idea that has been around for ages: When you set your mind on a single, concrete idea and all your mental energy converges on that idea, things happen that appear to be magical. Coincidence, after a while, does not appear to be such a coincidence.

I read a sports psychology book when I was 19 and told my dad that what I had just learned about was what I was going to do one day for the Steelers and Cowboys. (At the time the two were great rivals in the NFL.) One day as I returned home from working with the Cowboys, my dad reminded me of that dinner conversation. I never contacted either the Steelers or the Cowboys; they both somehow came to me *years later.*

If you get to a place where your thoughts are concrete, simple, and focused, and you take deliberate action, then your thoughts become realities.

When your thoughts are concrete, the message goes out and an answer will come. This situation will happen for you provided you keep changing and growing. If you get to a place where your thoughts are concrete, simple, and focused, and you take deliberate action, then your thoughts become realities.

THANKFUL ON CREDIT

A very powerful tool you can use is to be thankful in your meditation for what you have received *before* you have received it; this practice is called "being thankful on credit." In your mind you meditate on the gifts you have received and on the good fortune you have had—to receive them before you have received them. This is powerful visualization.

Being thankful on credit opens up an even more powerful energy coming to you and adds more positives to the picture. This sends the message that you are positive you are going to receive, and makes it more likely that you will.

> *You are positive you are going to receive, and makes it more likely that you will.*

JOURNALING

Mother Teresa said that when she thought of the masses, she did little, but when she thought of one, she always acted. Keep a journal or a notebook to write down what you intend the day to bring, what you intend to bring to the day, how you are going to specifically add value to someone else. Get a picture of adding value, doing one thing; then be thankful that this has happened before you leave your home.

When you come back at the end of the day, ask yourself how you did. The picture you had of the day, did it manifest itself? Did you show up in the picture and add value to others? Again, be thankful for what has happened, and then do it all over again the next day.

CHAPTER 7

The Action Season: You Do Not Get What You Want—You Get What You Deserve

*"We should work our process, not
the outcome of our processes."*

—W. Edwards Deming

The 1972 Pittsburgh Steelers were in a tough situation: fourth down, the last play of a playoff game, their season about to end, and the team about to lose by a few points to the Oakland Raiders. Quarterback Terry Bradshaw went back to pass and immediately had pass-rush pressure all around. In a desperate attempt, he threw the football with all his might down the field. It bounced off a player and fell into the hands of a full-striding Franco Harris, who came out of nowhere as he scooped up the ball to run for a touchdown. This win propelled the Steelers upward as one of the strongest franchises in all of sports and began that team's march to the first of four Super Bowls. This throw is still one of the most dramatic plays in football and is nicknamed "The Immaculate Reception."

Let's look at some of the possible mindsets of Franco Harris for that play. Did he possibly say to himself, "I will run down the side of the field; Bradshaw will run around like crazy, trying hard not to get sacked. He will then throw the ball, it will bounce off of someone's shoulder pads, I will scoop it up before it hits the ground, and then run to glory"? Did he say, "I will stand here in the backfield and dream that the ball will bounce to me or someone else and we will win; I do not have to do anything but dream it"? Or did he say to himself, "Run to where the ball will be and run hard"? Obviously, it was the last one.

> *Winning requires action,*
> *running, moving, and working.*

Winning requires action, running, moving, and working. Many people do not want to hear this, but you *have* to take action. Only the perplexed think they do not have to work, get up, and move toward the action. You can have a vision of a touchdown, but you also have to run hard to the ball. This is what you do during your "season."

THIS IS THE SEASON OF ACTION

There is a story of a minister who went to visit a member of his congregation who had recently bought a farm. The farmer had been working hard. The minister looked at the beautiful pastures and said, "This farm is beautiful; God has been really good to you with this farm." The owner said, "I am thankful for this farm, but you should have seen it when God had it all to himself."

Some people cannot embrace the fact that nothing works unless they do, believing instead that once they dream (or "place their order"), the "universe" will provide. If you are not ready to "pay," there *is* no future. If you order an oak tree, it does not arrive full grown. Once the time for "ordering" (the preseason) has been established in the subconscious, your focus must completely surrender to the process. You have work to do on your dream.

Once the time for "ordering" (the preseason) has been established in the subconscious, your focus must completely surrender to the process. You have work to do on your dream.

God gives you the tools, and you can order the seeds. You have to determine the cost and pay. You have to water the seeds and pull the weeds in your season of work. Now's the time when you care for your vision-come-to-life. You *deserve* the tree by establishing ownership when you oversee its growth, adhering to the process necessary for its daily care. Go fall in love with that tree by getting to know everything about it as it develops to maturity.

START WITH THE PROCESS

When I speak at conferences, the host company has its best salespeople present a panel discussion about their "process for success." Often they have very different paths on their journeys; yet they all succinctly describe these paths in a short period of time and in an understandable manner. They present an orderly packaged process in that seminar, and they can even "sell" it if necessary as their "special recipe." Their processes are so clear, and the best salespeople make them appear so simple that it is impossible *not* to see how they succeeded.

The first step in implementing your vision is developing a process, a step-by-step plan you use consistently everyday to get to the desired outcome. You can develop this plan in business and in your personal life—even if it's to be the most unbelievably great parent. An observer should be able to follow you around, recording the details of your plan. Even if you are teaching your family your vision of how to serve others, it should be clear enough to record.

> *The first step in implementing your vision is developing a process,*
> *a step-by-step plan you use consistently everyday to get to the desired outcome.*

You must work your dream—with consistency. You pay for your order with hard work. Yes, the work is uncomfortable, at least at first, but it's only uncomfortable, not awful, because you need *discipline.* Discipline—which requires that consistent and constant energy given—*will be* uncomfortable. But in life there are two types of pain—the pain of discipline and the pain of regret. Make your choice and run hard now in this season with discipline.

The word *consistency* is an exciting word; we love consistent friends, spouses, colleagues—consistent anything. The great figures in any field do the same thing over and over from a script without varying much. The profit-making restaurants, hair salons, churches—you name it—have a consistent way of doing whatever it is they do. In contrast, the restaurant that offers the best dish you ever tasted one week but a very mediocre dish the next will not be in service in a year or so. The one offering the same best dish each time will remain. Plan consistency into your season. Then nurture it as it grows.

START MAKING YOUR MOVE

A 14-year-old boy asked his mother if he could play a sport. However, he had one problem: He did not have a left arm. When his mother enrolled him in judo, his instructor taught him one move, telling him to master that one move. The instructor enrolled him in a tournament, and the boy won every match. Finally, he was in a championship bout with a brut. The referee went to the instructor before the bout and said, "You are going to get this boy killed."

The instructor replied, "The boy will be fine." The boy, too, said to his instructor, "You are going to get me killed." The instructor replied, "You will be just fine." The boy won the match! As the two were driving home, the boy asked, "Why did you do that to me? That guy was scary. I do not have a left arm and you taught me only one move." The instructor explained, "There is only one defense for that move—to grab the left arm!"

The secret is to learn your move until it is second nature to you. You do not need many moves; instead, perfect your move, the one that best matches you, and then keep making it. If it works for you, it is your plan for your season. You don't need to be fancy or complicated when you have a winning plan.

> *The secret is to learn your move until it is second nature to you. You do not need many moves; instead, perfect your move, the one that best matches you.*

Talking about his band's lead guitarist, Bono of U2 once said that he plays the guitar differently than anyone else in the world. His playing is unique, and there is nobody like him. You and your move are unique. There is nobody else like you. Therefore, identify your move, master it, and keep it as your special move.

NOW STAY ON THE PROCESS

When my close friend got cancer, he was told he had less than a 50-percent chance to beat it. He told me he felt that if he did not hit a breaking point and could keep from getting discouraged, and instead kept punching for the sake of his wife and son, then he would be "okay." But if he ever surrendered "silently," he would be gone quickly. It took some time, but he won that fight.

Discouragement is a state in which someone quits his or her process, or at least goes through the motions with a lot less energy. The person is feeling inadequate or that he or she will never receive a payoff. This situation happens in every area of life, and you seldom hear this surrender. Someone just slips silently away.

SET UP AN INTERNAL VOCABULARY OF
ENCOURAGEMENT

What sets up discouragement? If we praise ourselves and others when there are results, what happens when we are giving our all in our efforts but yet see no results? We get discouraged, and the process then could slip into silent surrender. But if we acknowledge when we are doing better, showing improvement, performing the steps, and giving the proper effort, then we don't need to be discouraged. These factors—showing improvement and adherence to a process—give the result, not praise, for achievement.

Here are some phrases you can use to talk to yourself, to "self-coach":

I am making improvements at _____

_____ .

It appears I have a talent for _____

_____ .

I really enjoyed myself in the area of _____

_____ .

I am not pleased, but I can do _____

_____ ,

which will allow me to be pleased.

I have confidence in my judgment of _____

_____ .

I can handle _____

_____ .

Some psychologists say that more than 75 percent of what we say to ourselves is negative. I am not simply trying to champion positive self-talk. Instead, I am trying to bring about an internal vocabulary of encouragement—phrases you say to yourself that keep you on the move and on-process. This type of "process focusing" is concrete and helps you get better. Do the steps and acknowledge the areas where you are enjoying yourself.

> *I am trying to bring about an internal vocabulary of encouragement— phrases you say to yourself that keep you on the move and on-process.*

Words such as *winning* and *goal*—although good concepts indeed—are too abstract when trying to get to *the doing*—to taking effective action. Many times, athletes try to command their bodies to win, but their bodies are confused by the abstract terminology. Winning is not an action. Winning is an outcome of sustained effective action. However, when athletes command their bodies to perform a certain action, such as *looking* the ball into their hands, they succeed—they catch the ball. If they do that command enough—they catch the ball enough—they win!

Think these phrases, practice them, and say them out loud. (There are plenty more in the chapter at the end of the book.) If you let "discouragement language" get in your head and take over, you will abandon your process and surrender silently.

TOO HARD TO PLAY HARD

I have a friend who has developed many top college quarterbacks who have gone to play in the NFL. One of his favorite sayings is, "Quarterback is too hard to play hard." In other words, when someone is *doing* too much or doing *more* than his process can handle—and thus is forcing something to happen, as opposed to letting it happen—then it *never* happens.

You name it—marriage, parenting, teaching, stock-brokering—all are too hard to play hard. All you have to do is get your process in front of you and let it happen, not force it to happen. In other words, play easy. Reggie Jackson, one of the greatest hitters to ever play the game of baseball, would say out loud after he struck out, "I am reminded that when we lose and I strike out, a billion people in China don't care." Jackson is reminding us to get over ourselves and not take ourselves too seriously. Truly successful people have an ease and grace about them—they make it look easy. After you declare your process, "it" should all be "easy does it."

A FOCUS

I was working with Rutgers University when the team was playing the largest ESPN college football game to be broadcast to date. The team was trying to get to its first bowl game and was playing on a Thursday night against the number-two team in the country, Louisville. With Rutgers down 21–0, a Rutgers defensive tackle made a sack, then looked over at our sideline and started the "chopping wood" signal, thus sending the message that he was not worried about the score.

Similar to "felling a tree," he was focusing on the task at hand, not the scoreboard. He was just chopping away. Near the end of the game, the score was tied, and Rutgers had to kick a field goal to win the game. When the kicker missed, the camera zoomed over to the head coach—and he just made a chopping motion. It turned out that Louisville was offside on that field-goal attempt, so Rutgers got to try the field goal again—and this time won the game!

Do you have a gesture that means you're staying on-process? Many have gestures that show the world where to go and say that they quit. A "focus gesture" is the same thing in reverse. Do you have a one that says, "I am still in the game, so hang in there with me"?

People often ask me what my focus phrase is. My phrase came from an experience many years ago. A lawn company looked at my yard to see if they could "tidy it up" a bit. But they shook their heads and drove away without even saying good-bye. So I went across the street to an old farmer, Jake, to ask if he had a tip for me about my lawn. He did, telling me to "keep planting grass; don't pull weeds."

It was perfect. I had a great yard by the time I moved. When my children are struggling, I go plant seeds; when business turns a little slow, I plant seeds; when I get lonely, I plant a few seeds. Not all the seeds catch, but eventually I have a number of nice lawns. I always tell myself, "Keep planting grass."

WHAT IS DETERMINATION?

David Wells was warming up to pitch for the New York Yankees when a fan of the opposing team screamed, "Hey, Wells, your mother sucks." Wells had buried his mother the week before and had just returned to the pitching rotation. In the dugout before the game, he thought of his mother and of his anger with this inconsiderate fan. He gave up a number of runs and hits in the first inning because he was angry and unfocused, but manager Joe Torre did not pull him. Finally, he pitched out of the inning, sat alone on the bench, and had a conversation with himself. He told himself he was not going to surrender to that fan, and he was going to throw the ball, one pitch at a time, to the catcher's glove, with all he had, and he was dedicating the rest of the game to his mother.

From then on, he did not give up one hit, and the Yankees won. Afterward at the press conference, Wells told the reporters what had happened, how he initially handled it, and eventually responded: "To the guy who had the rude comment about my mother, thank you. I guess in some strange way you are responsible for this great day."

Obstacles, struggles, and setbacks are nothing more than a challenge for you to respond to with focused energy.

The obstacles, struggles, and setbacks are nothing more than a challenge for you to respond to with focused energy—one pitch, one sale, one interaction with your child, or one prayer at a time. At the end of the day, you owe whatever propelled you to that state—disguised as a rude fan, insurmountable obstacle, crushing divorce—a thank-you for kicking it all off and allowing you to see what you are really made of.

A GREAT EXAMPLE OF A LIFE OF
PROCESS

A man came up to me with an unbelievable story when I was speaking in Red Bank, New Jersey. Having three kids from his first marriage—ages 10, 12, and 18—he remarried at 52. His second wife was 40. When she got pregnant, it threw him for a loop. Everyday he looked out of his New York City office, repeating, "I don't need this. I am going to have to work until I am 90." Almost like a self-fulfilling prophesy, his wife had twin boys. He eventually quit on his wife, on the two kids, even on his job as a New York City stockbroker.

This discouragement went on for some time— a silent surrender—until one day, 18 months later, one of his twin sons fell into a pond...and drowned. When the mother got there, all that was sticking out of the water was one tennis shoe. She screamed. The father immediately pulled his son from the water and performed CPR on his lifeless body. Miraculously, he came back to life. They rushed the little boy to the emergency room. The doctor asked where the dad got his CPR training, but the dad said he didn't have any.

The doctor, in his 38 years of experience with these kind of cases, said that in every previous case the child had brain damage and broken ribs, but this child was fine. The family soon took him home.

I've become friends with this man; his plan now is to be the best husband, father, and stockbroker he can be with complete surrender to the process—and whatever comes, comes. He is number one in performance at his broker/dealer firm, and his wife says he is an amazing father and husband—all for one reason: He is free. All he can do anything about is to focus on the process. He has a great marriage, family, and career because he deserves it.

You never get what you want. Instead, you always get what you deserve—what you make happen with your process.

You never get what you want. Instead, you always get what you deserve—what you make happen with your process. The ball is in your arms. Run hard with it. Run with consistency and discipline and your distinctive plan in your season.

CHAPTER 8

The Playoffs

*"All we have to do is to decide what
to do with the time given to us."*

—J.R.R. Tolkien

When I finished my doctorate, I started my career in the wellness division of a hospital. After my shift one warm Fall night, I stood outside my car, talking to a young medical doctor who started to work the same day I did. I asked him, "When did you become a doctor?" His answer floored me. He said, "I was a doctor as long as I can remember, even as a small child. I eventually went to school and got a piece of paper to make it official." Or in other words: It happens over a long period of time, all of a sudden.

These two phrases get linked together strangely as one describes the way this process of success ultimately takes place. There comes a time when what you are trying to obtain is really here, when the growth you seek has arrived. It is not that you "think" it is going to happen, but rather that now you-know-that-you know-that-you-know. You have thought your dream into reality. It involves looking to a time you know will arrive and then recognizing its arrival so that you can claim what you have earned that is now yours.

There comes a time when what you are
trying to obtain is really here, when
the growth you seek has arrived.

When I was working with the University of
Miami football team, we were playing the University of Nebraska in the Rose Bowl for the
National Championship. Coming out onto the
field to play, the Nebraska team was very demonstrative. Most of the people in the stands from
Nebraska were loud, too, but Miami was very
quiet. Nebraska had just lost a game to the University of Colorado, but Miami was on a bit of
a winning streak. Larry Coker, then the head
coach of Miami, an extremely humble, good
man, came over to me, watching the quiet business-like approach of the team, and said, "When
they get like this, it is scary, not for us, but for
whoever is out there with them. Here comes a
big day." Larry is anything but cocky. Yet, he was
wise enough to watch the team and observe that
they "knew that they knew." That day Miami
claimed the National Championship.

This story is not about one football team, but about every champion, gold-medal winner, team, family, business—you name it. They have something they have worked for, and they know it has arrived before it has arrived. Change has come. That winning season is here. When there is a not knowing, the arrogance or panic is evident; others can tell. But a receiver of the genuine knows its arrival, too, and when you are around the "real deal," that person's confidence is amazing. They know they belong in the "playoffs" of life.

CLAIM IT

Two weeks after September 11 (yes, that one), I went down to speak to the Miami Dolphins and stayed for their game against the Oakland Raiders. This was the first week of games after the terrorist attacks, because games had been canceled the week before. In that game, starting quarterback Jay Fiedler threw two interceptions, and 60,000 people booed him. The Raiders hit him hard with about a minute and a half to go, and he seemed not to know where he was. The coaches even tried to pull him out of the game.

However, with just seconds to go in the game, Jay scrambled and scored the winning touchdown. The next week, a picture of him extended over the goal line was the front cover of *Sport Illustrated.*

Jay went to Dartmouth. His roommate at Dartmouth worked for Cantor Fitzgerald, a financial company in the World Trade Center that lost more than 700 people in the attacks. Jay's friend worked Tokyo business hours, and he actually walked out of the World Trade Center minutes before the attacks started. When he got home that day, his first call was to Jay. The conversation he had with Jay was a "claim it" one. He said, "The terrorists will not terrorize me. I will miss my lost friends and then reclaim who I am and then some."

Jay went into the game with that same mindset; at the beginning of that long week, he placed a vision in his head of who *he* was going to be, told his close teammates who that was, worked hard all week and during the game for it, and now with a minute and a half until the clock ran out, he was going to claim what he had earned and who he now was as a result of growth from that awful event. The claiming was the completion step in the cycle.

> *Forward motion, together with the claiming and ownership of all that has been earned, happens over time.*

When growing into a new station in life is real, it takes time. Forward motion, together with the claiming and ownership of all that has been earned, happens over time. When a cycle of change and growth is nearing completion, you "rev up" and claim as yours that which you have earned. The claiming is the reward ceremony. You walk up onstage and collect the prize; you put on the cap and gown and receive the diploma.

Sometimes others may boo. Perhaps they think you just got lucky. They may not know that luck must be earned. They may not understand that success happens over a long period of time—all of a sudden. They may not see the real prize, or know the "real deal," but you do and you must rev up to claim it.

If you have not earned the championship, the wealth, or the peace, and are not someone who is worthy in your own view of receiving it, you may fool others but ultimately not yourself. You can't fake you. You'll know you're not playoff material yet. You'll know you have more work to do.

Remember you do not "get" wealth; instead, you simply become someone who offers value to others and they return the blessings.

In this process of change and growth, any difficulty will serve a useful purpose of teaching you where you need to sustain or improve your effort.

Remember you do not "get" wealth; instead, you simply become someone who offers value to others and they return the blessings. It is the same with your health. Give value to your body, and your body will return the blessings. Wealth, health, and happiness are outward manifestations that mirror who you have become and what you have worked for over time. It is what we call "an inside job!"

CHAPTER 9

The Off-Season

*"Rest when you are weary. Refresh and
renew yourself, your body, your mind,
your spirit. Then get back to work."*

—*Ralph Marsten*

One Saturday when I was working for the Pittsburgh Steelers, the announcers for the game being played the next day wandered into the training room where I was hanging out. One of the announcers, Sam Wyche, who previously was head coach of the Cincinnati Bengals and the Tampa Bay Buccaneers, wanted to talk with a Steelers player who played for him in Tampa. The player, Courtney Hawkins, was being treated for an injury, so Wyche and I had some time on our hands to talk.

When Wyche was with the Bengals, the team went to the Super Bowl, so I took the opportunity to ask him what factors were involved. He said there was one major factor. They started their Super Bowl year with a dismal record, and after another early season loss, the owner of the team said he wanted Wyche and every other coach in his office at 6 p.m. with their playbooks. Sam said he was sure they were all being fired. When they walked in, the owner said, "I want every one of you out of here and home at six o'clock at the latest—every one of you. And when you leave, I want you to place your playbook in here so you do not go home to work." Then Wyche said, "Thus we went to the Super Bowl."

Americans have no idea how to rest, and the only way most can rest is when it is mandated. We cannot get back in harmony with ourselves and our lives and we will remain "out of sync" without rest. When you get a vision, you should not ignore it, but rather hold it in a pure, uncluttered state of mind, do the work to make it happen, and most importantly, live in a rhythm. All of nature, including man, lives in a rhythm. That is the reason why the plant that lies dormant in the winter can flourish in the spring; it is in its rhythm. It knows the time for every purpose when in its particular season; therefore, it knows when to rest. However, man has a capacity for awareness and as a result has the possibility of choice. So unlike a plant, we must choose the rhythm.

> *We cannot get back in harmony with ourselves and our lives and we will remain "out of sync" without rest.*

French mathematician and philosopher Pascal once said that all of man's difficulties come from his inability to sit quietly for 20 minutes. It definitely comes from his difficulty to sit quietly at all. My neighbor is a physician, and we were discussing interns. He said so many of them gain weight because they have never worked long shifts before and therefore are not getting their needs met for quiet downtime, so they substitute food. In our hurry, it seems sickness of relentless activity and overpacked schedules has translated into many other sicknesses as well, such as anxiety, depression, overeating, you name it. I have heard motivational speakers say, "You can rest when you are dead." Well, if you follow that advice, you may get to rest a lot quicker than you anticipated. Death is often your body's way of saying, "Slow down."

Moreover, when we are in the action phase, we are usually operating at about two-thirds of our best if we never take a break. We are not really able to fully engage because we are not really able to be "in the moment"; the mind is not able to get the "housecleaning" it gets when it rests, so it is only partially engaged. Many current studies state that we need at least seven-and-a-half hours of sleep each night, and not many people can say they get even this much, besides taking a proper break now and then. Taking a break—not just keeping a Sabbath, but taking a sabbatical—is not a lifestyle suggestion but a "living fully" requirement. It is a season requirement. It fulfills the cycle of change our bodies need.

According to certain studies, some children who have attention deficit disorder are effectively being treated by allowing them to sit quietly in a meditative state—it is as effective in some cases as medication. For the same reason, I found that when I started jogging one hour a day during college, my academic performance went way up, because running was my meditation. The world as we know it has attention deficit disorder.

I used to think it was just men, but women these days are almost as bad; it is everyone's caused-by-hurry-cannot-take-a-break sickness. The answer, not just for children, is a quiet break.

The off-season is a time when you recapture your soul. If you sell it during the season, this is the time when you buy it back.

The off-season is a time when you recapture your soul. If you sell it during the season, this is the time when you buy it back. The way of nature is to take a period for re-creation—it allows you to perform effectively and enjoy your performance much more. I am sure that this off-season is a necessity of human nature and your personal rhythm. Let's face it: Your spirit and probably your health will wither without an off-season because this need is deeply embedded in your nature. And more unnatural is what you have become—a 24/7, 365-days-year, habitual player with a constant playing season. Such a schedule will make it all the harder for you to accept that you need downtime. Even if you do not accept this, the denied facts remain.

MY WISH

Take a day to go on a walk with your family, a friend, or alone. There is nothing like a 20-minute walk. In fact, I trust the thoughts I get when I'm in motion much more than the ones I get while standing still. There is magic in putting your body in peaceful motion.

Get a massage, take a nap, take a long bath, or walk barefoot in your backyard. Give your body a break. Give your mind a break by turning off the phone.

Go see a friend, sit down face-to-face and talk—no timetable, just talk. Remember the fun times you had with him or her, especially a friend you grew up with. Or get out the home movies of old vacations and reminisce about them with a friend or your family.

Create an "off-season" box and place the box inside your front door. Write on pieces of paper all the "things" of the season you must contend with and place the papers in the box. Let them sit in there for the off-season. If you start to address these concerns during this time of rest, remind yourself that they are in the box and you will take care of them in the upcoming preseason.

> *If you are not in harmony with the rhythm of things, there are consequences.*

You are a creation of nature, living with the rest of creation. Everything around you that is not man-made is in a rhythm. You are, too, but you are also free to make choices. If you are not in harmony with the rhythm of things, there are consequences. Choose to be a spiritual being having a human experience, and get in rhythm. *Now after your rest, you are ready to plan, create, and start y*our preseason again.

CHAPTER 10

Speaking Out: Heart Song Catalogue of Catchphrases

*"The written word can be erased—
not so with the spoken word."*

—*Author unknown*

I am now asking you to do something different and unorthodox: to talk out loud so your heart can hear you. Although I have found no books today suggesting this behavior, I know there is magic in speaking out loud. Does it mean that you are crazy if you walk around saying these recommended phrases out loud? Maybe, but what if you are *too* sane now? What is all the big deal about being sane? It is overrated. I would rather be excited, alive, fighting the good fight than sane. I know sane people who wouldn't dare any of these techniques, but, please, are they not boring?

What is all the big deal about being sane?
It is overrated. I would rather be excited,
alive, fighting the good fight than sane.

By way of example, in the 2008 Super Bowl, Michael Strahan stood on the sidelines in the fourth quarter addressing his New York Giants team: "The final score of this game is 17–14. Believe that and it will happen." At the time they were losing 14–10. The team must have believed, because 17–14 *was* the final score and his New York Giants won. So we see here that three steps make up undertaking the seemingly impossible:

1. **Thinking it**.

2. **Speaking it**.

3. **Acting it**.

Life and death are in the tongue; it's powerful beyond measure. However, few pay attention to the spoken word. If you really want to do something amazing, you have to listen to your words because they manifest miracles. See the event in your mind, make it happen there, declare it out loud, and know it is going to happen.

Now try this. For a moment, quietly count backward in your mind from 10 to 1. Midway through your count, at about number 5, say your name out loud. Did you keep on counting after you said it? I have never heard a person say, "Yes, I continued to count." People stop counting right there. When you say something out loud, everything in you stops to listen to what you are saying. If you really understand this phenomenon and practice saying things *out loud* that inspire you and cause you to focus, then you never need any person but yourself to be there for you to know what to do.

> *When you say something out loud, everything in you stops to listen to what you are saying.*

When I interview college players wanting to enter the NFL, I asked if they are leaders. Often they answer, "I lead by example." I always think, "How convenient; nobody knows what you think because you don't open your mouth." Yes, you need to be an example, but you must also have a vision you speak out about. Otherwise, the model is incomplete. There is more to being a leader than setting an example; spoken words are important, too.

> *There is more to being a leader than setting an example; spoken words are important, too.*

You must talk loud enough for at least "you" to hear your vision, if not for the entire world to hear it. To speak your vision takes courage, boldness, and maybe even a little wildness, because your tongue is the "pen" you need to write with on the tablet of your heart—and the heart of others. When you speak it, the vision becomes established like dry ink. Your spoken words are your individualized mission statement.

To begin, say "I quit worrying about sane." Try it now. Walk around talking to yourself out loud; let them call you crazy. By doing this, you will find power and forces acting on your behalf. Go ahead and say what the final score is, that you and your team are the winner, even when you are losing in the fourth quarter. Speak the dream into existence.

Read through the "Heart Song Catalogue of Catchphrases" that follow. Choose a couple phrases. Start saying them out loud and watch the spoken word call forth reality. If you don't like any of these phrases, create your own (maybe something a parent or old friend told you). Then speak your phrase. When your dream does materialize, watch the look on the faces of the people who heard you walking around talking to yourself. Who is crazy now? Speak your dream into life.

Here are a few heart song catchphrases to get you started.

ANTI-FEAR HEART SONGS

Trust—This word shows faith, meaning you expect good things to happen; you are calling agents of good, posturing for blessings to come, even expecting good. Saying it means "I know that I know that I know." Spoken out loud, *trust* keeps all your senses up, looking for victory. It keeps the mind quiet, ending its chattering judgment.

Whatever comes to me, I will overcome—It is childish to think a challenge will not come your way in some form sooner or later. But it is easy to get the childish notion that we are cursed because "something" has happened to us. Remember that things eventually happen to everyone. You were built to last longer than any challenge, so keep saying this phrase out loud until you believe the truth: that you are bigger than the challenge.

I have a vision—If you have a vision, hold it, trust it, and do not allow anything to intrude on it that makes you surrender. It will happen. Remember that a vision is not a vision until it is tested. Make your vision last longer than your fear.

> *Remember that a vision is not a vision until it is tested. Make your vision last longer than your fear.*

ANTI-WORRY HEART SONGS

Regardless of circumstances, I feast—Many people argue about why they should have anxiety and fear in their lives. If you argue they should not, they will say you do not completely understand their circumstance. They believe that the circumstance is making them anxious, rather than their mindset. Therefore, this phrase is a great one to say out loud; it tells the heart to hear that the circumstance does not matter and that you will win because you do not live in circumstance but in vision. And oh yes—you still have to do the work to change and grow.

I find answers and answers find me—When someone has a problem, it does not seem like such a problem once he or she begins solving it. The "problem" with a problem arises when people want to keep studying it rather than going forward with possible solutions. The problem needs to be studied, but not *overstudied.* Have you ever held a problem in your consciousness, or contemplated it for a while, and then let it go; or maybe prayed about it, and then your mind woke up, saying, "I think I have a solution here"? That happens because you were finally open to the solution. At the point of this "wakeup call," you are probably not sure if you found the solution or if the solution found you.

PHRASES TO FEND OFF ANGER

If I am easy going, life is easy—This is my mission statement every time I walk through the doors of an airport. Many times travelers—tired, away from their families—can be an angry group, and because of this challenge, I need a vision or else I'll join them. I envision having a great trip, meeting cool people, helping others, and serving life.

And you know what happens? My trips turn out pretty much like the vision. Try it wherever you go—you'll like the way you feel.

I will expect people to be who they are—A woman came to me for counseling, saying she was mad at her husband because he didn't speak to her, but then she went on to say that he never had! No matter who they are—boss, employee, lover, in-law—expect people to be who they are, not who you have decided they should be—and probably never were. Now watch your anger leave.

PHRASES TO EASE THE HARD

I expect there to be challenges, so I will bring the best me—When I work with National Football League players, they often say, "The guy opposite of me on the other team is good. I expect him to be, so I will not take any plays 'off.' I will bring the best me to each play." There is a misconception that athletes "make big plays." Instead, the big play shows up when it is ready to show up, and the great athletes know that they have to be present and show up when that opportunity arrives. It is the player who quits or takes a play off because it is "hard" who will miss the opportunity.

> *The big play shows up when it is ready to show up, and the great athletes know that they have to be present and show up when that opportunity arrives.*

Parenting, marriage, sales, leadership—all of it is hard. However, a great moment or opportunity shows up when it is ready, and you have to be present at that time. If something is hard, so be it. You do not back down; you always bring the best *you* to every moment.

I do not surrender to the greatest temptation— The greatest temptation is self-pity. With self-pity, you are not thinking something is just hard, but rather that something is *too* hard. It is beyond you; it is more than you can handle. Be careful when you tell yourself that something in your opinion is too hard, because you tend to believe yourself.

By my steadfastness and patient endurance, I will win—Almost everything in life is a marathon, and if you endure and keep giving steadfast energy, even though it is tough, you will win. The challenge is that sometimes people feel things are too hard and curl themselves into a ball. If you are supposed to do a sales presentation, for instance, say to yourself, "This room must be full of blessings I cannot see, because I am scheduled to give this presentation…and here it goes." Keep doing without judging, and the *hard* will dissolve.

ANTI-REJECTION PHRASES

My worth cannot be changed by opinion—You have to uncouple your self-worth from the "good opinion" of others. If you don't, you will lose so much energy you will never be able to manifest your vision. You will have a new, more-consuming vision of getting everybody to like you. This will begin to displace your grand vision and you will fail at both.

Separate the "who" from the "do"—If you receive feedback that you should do something different or you did something wrong, that does not mean *you* are wrong or your path is wrong. It means you received feedback—that's all. If you trust the person giving the feedback, you can change your process, but use caution. You can have people who you respect provide feedback, but not judge you or the dream as wrong.

Some people offer their opinion because they love to offer their opinion and hear their own voice, although they pretend they are offering it because they care. Some others think you need their opinion or at least they are entitled to give it. Then others actually do care and may think they should help you. This thinking is fine, especially if they are accomplished in your area. But remember the difference between opinion and permission. You are not seeking permission from others. This is *your* dream. Do not lose sight of it lightly.

This dream has chosen me—People get discouraged because they wonder if they are doing the
right thing when they face a challenge. If you are
passionately pursuing your dream, in a strange
way the *dream* has chosen you. You probably
have certain gifts and interests, and somehow
this idea has popped into your head and you're
not even sure how. This enigma is the beauty of a
dream. So do not think, "Should I do this thing,
because I am getting discouraged?" Rather,
knowing that the dream "found" you, be encour-
aged and keep moving boldly through the seasons of fulfillment.

SONGS TO PREVENT LAZINESS AND
PASSIVITY

My reward is already here—Saying this out loud
can make you move. It lets your body know that
you are going out to collect what you have earned
and now belongs to you. This phrase releases
energy throughout your body like it is Christmas morning: you are walking with expectation.
When people walk around thinking "What is the
use?," there usually isn't one for them.

I work for my own support—We do not get what we need but rather what we have earned. There is nothing like knowing you earned the reward, that your vision is something you paid for in advance. Before you get it, you earn it and then deserve it. To know you are going out every day, not surrendering to passivity, gives you the knowledge that you deserve your vision and that you can support *you*. Your vote is the most important vote you can get. In this sense, you deserve what you get—totally.

> *There is nothing like knowing you earned the reward, that your vision is something you paid for in advance.*

My hands are not idle—Keep giving your body outward commands that it is to be in motion; do not let any part of your body think it can be lazy and passive. When you command this, your body responds. Stay in motion because as the saying "use it, or lose it" definitely applies to your body.

PHRASES FOR PATIENCE

Rain will come, so prepare the fields—The vision, dream, and blessing come when they are ready; in the meantime, do your part: prepare the fields. Seeds do not reach their glorious potential planted in barren soil. Neither do dreams. Your mind, body, and soul are the soil that gives life to the seeds of your dream. In fact, it is not the dream that is not ready; mostly the garden and gardener are not. Don't quit doing your work of preparing for and expecting to receive.

Better is the ending than the beginning—When you say this phrase, you are informing the heart that the end reward is coming, so you need to "finish" the job. You must keep on keeping on. You have to stay on the path and know that you will receive again—*whenever* that might be.

I will expect situations to be what they are— An employer once told me he hires people who were in the military because they understand that part of any job stinks. (According to him, 20 percent of a job stinks.) They do not get angry, and can see that the rest of the job is rather good. No matter what you do, some of it is not fun. For example, I loved having babies, but do not miss changing diapers. Align your expectations with reality; expect parts of what you do to be just what they are and quit expecting them to be different from what they are.

Align your expectations with reality; expect parts of what you do to be just what they are and quit expecting them to be different from what they are.

PHRASES AGAINST WATERING DOWN
YOUR DREAM

*I was born to play big. I am allowed to dream anything I want, so it might as well be big—*There are big plans for you. Someone has to have a big dream, so why not you? Once you start to believe and refuse to yield, you will achieve your dream. Don't "dummy down" your vision. You might find a cure, touch a heart, or start a center. Start big and finish big. How many people will miss an opportunity for something great if you surrender now?

*I do not compromise—*There is a time to compromise—in financial deals or over family vacation sites—but not when it comes to your vision.

* * * * *

Keep dreaming and visualizing. Take action and keep practicing. Keep score and measure your progress. Keep on keeping on, and I'll see you at the winner's table.

Index

FINANCIAL TIMES

In an increasingly competitive world, it is quality of thinking that gives an edge—an idea that opens new doors, a technique that solves a problem, or an insight that simply helps make sense of it all.

We work with leading authors in the various arenas of business and finance to bring cutting-edge thinking and best-learning practices to a global market.

It is our goal to create world-class print publications and electronic products that give readers knowledge and understanding that can then be applied, whether studying or at work.

To find out more about our business products, you can visit us at www.ftpress.com.